Janice VanCleave's

Engineering
for Every Kid

Other Titles by Janice VanCleave

Science for Every Kid series:
Janice VanCleave's Astronomy for Every Kid
Janice VanCleave's Biology for Every Kid
Janice VanCleave's Chemistry for Every Kid
Janice VanCleave's Constellations for Every Kid
Janice VanCleave's Dinosaurs for Every Kid
Janice VanCleave's Earth Science for Every Kid
Janice VanCleave's Ecology for Every Kid
Janice VanCleave's Energy for Every Kid
Janice VanCleave's Food and Nutrition for Every Kid
Janice VanCleave's Geography for Every Kid
Janice VanCleave's Geometry for Every Kid
Janice VanCleave's The Human Body for Every Kid
Janice VanCleave's Math for Every Kid
Janice VanCleave's Oceans for Every Kid
Janice VanCleave's Physics for Every Kid

Spectacular Science Projects series:
Janice VanCleave's Animals
Janice VanCleave's Earthquakes
Janice VanCleave's Electricity
Janice VanCleave's Gravity
Janice VanCleave's Insects and Spiders
Janice VanCleave's Machines
Janice VanCleave's Magnets
Janice VanCleave's Microscopes and Magnifying Lenses
Janice VanCleave's Molecules
Janice VanCleave's Plants
Janice VanCleave's Rocks and Minerals
Janice VanCleave's Solar System
Janice VanCleave's Volcanoes
Janice VanCleave's Weather

Also:
Janice VanCleave's 200 Gooey, Slippery, Slimy, Weird, and Fun Experiments
Janice VanCleave's 201 Awesome, Magical, Bizarre, and Incredible Experiments
Janice VanCleave's 202 Oozing, Bubbling, Dripping, and Bouncing Experiments
Janice VanCleave's 203 Icy, Freezing, Frosty, and Cool Experiments
Janice VanCleave's 204 Sticky, Gloppy, Wacky, and Wonderful Experiments
Janice VanCleave's Great Science Project Ideas from Real Kids
Janice VanCleave's Guide to the Best Science Fair Projects
Janice VanCleave's Guide to More of the Best Science Fair Projects
Janice VanCleave's Science Around the Year
Janice VanCleave's Science Through the Ages
Janice VanCleave's Scientists
Janice VanCleave's Science Around the World

JB JOSSEY-BASS

Janice VanCleave's

Engineering for Every Kid

Easy Activities That Make Learning Science Fun

Janice VanCleave

BICENTENNIAL
BICENTENNIAL
1807
WILEY
2007
BICENTENNIAL
BICENTENNIAL

John Wiley & Sons, Inc.

Published by Jossey-Bass
A Wiley Imprint
989 Market Street, San Francisco, CA 94103-1741
www.josseybass.com

Wiley Bicentennial Logo: Richard J. Pacifico

The publisher and the author have made every reasonable effort to insure that the experiments and activities in the book are safe when conducted as instructed but assume no responsibility for any damage caused or sustained while performing the experiments or activities in this book. Parents, guardians, and/or teachers should supervise young readers who undertake the experiments and activities in this book.

Jossey-Bass books and products are available through most bookstores. To contact Jossey-Bass directly call our Customer Care Department within the U.S. at 800-956-7739, outside the U.S. at 317-572-3986, or fax 317-572-4002.

Jossey-Bass also publishes its books in a variety of electronic formats. Some content that appears in print may not be available in electronic books.

Library of Congress Cataloging-in-Publication Data

VanCleave, Janice Pratt.
 Janice VanCleave's engineering for every kid : easy activities that make learning science fun / Janice VanCleave. — 1st ed.
  p. cm. — (Science for every kid)
 Includes index.
 ISBN 978-0-471-47182-0 (pbk.)
 1. Engineering—Experiments—Juvenile literature. 2. Science—Experiments—Juvenile literature. I. Title. II. Series: VanCleave, Janice Pratt. Janice VanCleave science for every kid series.
 TA149.V36 2006
 620.0078—dc22

2006010540

Printed in the United States of America
first edition

10 9 8 7 6 5 4 3 2 1

This book is dedicated to a very loving lady
and a special person in my life:
my daughter Ginger Russell.

Contents

viii   **Contents**

Introduction

This is a basic book about engineering that is designed to teach facts, concepts, and problem-solving strategies. Each section introduces concepts about engineering that make learning useful and fun.

Engineering is the application of science, mathematics, and experience to produce a thing or a process that is useful. Engineering is neither more nor less important than science, just different. The basic objective of science is to discover the composition and behavior of the physical world; that is, **science** is a study of the natural world. The basic objective of engineering is to use scientific principles and methods to produce useful devices and services that serve humankind.

Examples of the work of engineers include making things like buildings, bridges, and airplanes and designing useful services, such as ways to clean up an oil spill in the ocean or to keep flood waters out of low-lying areas. Since useful things and processes must "obey" the laws of nature, engineers must understand and use these laws. Although engineering and science are two separate fields of study, in practice the work of real-world scientists and real-world engineers overlaps to some degree. For example, scientists use engineering ideas when they design instruments for experiments, and engineers use scientific experiments when they test the laws of nature in order to develop new things.

This book will not provide all the answers about engineering, but it will offer keys to understanding more about the work of engineers. It will guide you to answering questions such as,

What wing shape gives airplanes their lift? How does knowledge about density help determine the best materials for fire control? What types of instruments do meteorological engineers design and test?

This book is designed to teach engineering concepts so that they can be applied to many situations. The problems, experiments, and other activities are easy to understand. One of the main objectives of the book is to make learning about engineering *fun*.

How to Use This Book

Read each chapter slowly and follow procedures carefully. New terms are boldfaced and defined in the text when first introduced. So if you do not read the chapters in order, you may need to look in the Glossary for unfamiliar science terms. The format for each section is:

- **What You Need to Know:** Background information and an explanation of terms.

- **Exercises:** Questions to be answered or situations to be solved using the information from What You Need to Know.

- **Activity:** A project to allow you to apply the skill to a problem-solving situation in the real world.

- **Solutions to Exercises:** Step-by-step instructions for solving the Exercises.

All **boldfaced** terms are defined in the Glossary at the end of the book. Be sure to flip back to the Glossary as often as you need to, making each term part of your personal vocabulary.

General Instructions for the Exercises

1. Study each problem and solution carefully by reading it through once or twice before answering.

2. Check your answers in the Solutions to Exercises to evaluate your work.

3. Do the work again if any of your answers are incorrect.

General Instructions for the Activities

1. Read each activity completely before starting.

2. Collect needed supplies. You will have less frustration and more fun if all the necessary materials for the activities are ready before you start. You lose your train of thought when you have to stop and search for supplies.

3. Do not rush through the activity. Follow each step very carefully; never skip steps, and do not add your own. Safety is of utmost importance, and by reading each activity before starting, then following the instructions exactly, you can feel confident that no unexpected results will occur.

4. Observe. If your results are not the same as described in the activity, carefully reread the instructions and start over from step 1.

1
Push and Pull
Structural Engineering

What You Need to Know

Structural engineering is the branch of engineering concerned with the design and construction of all types of structures such as bridges, buildings, dams, tunnels, power plants, offshore drilling platforms, and space satellites. Structural engineers research the forces that will affect the structure, then develop a design that allows it to withstand these forces.

A **force** is a push or a pull on an object. The two basic forces on a structure are **lateral forces** (forces directed at the side of a structure) and **vertical forces** (forces directed up or down on a structure). Lateral forces on a structure might include **wind** (moving air).

The main vertical force on a structure is **gravity** (force pulling an object downward, which is toward the center of Earth). **Weight** is the measure of the force of gravity on an object. The weight of an object depends on **mass**, which is the amount of substance in the object. The greater the mass, the greater the weight; thus, the greater the force of gravity.

Engineers refer to the gravity force acting on a structure as the sum of its dead and live forces. **Dead forces** are the weight of the permanent parts making up the structure. In a building, dead forces include the weight of the walls, floors, and roof. **Live forces** are the weight of temporary objects in or on a structure. In a building, live forces include the weight of people, furniture, and snow on the roof. In the figure, live forces include the weight of the wagon, the child, and the boy; dead forces include all the parts making up the bridge. The total gravity force acting on the bridge is shown by the arrow directed downward.

Since shapes of materials affect their strength, structural engineers must consider what shapes to use in designing structures that will stand up to both lateral and vertical forces.

Exercises

1. In a building, which choice represents a live force?

    a. floors

    b. windows

    c. desk

2. Which force in the figure, A, B, or C, is the lateral force?

Activity: SHAPELY

Purpose To determine how the shape of a material can make it stronger.

Materials   2 books of equal thickness
　　　　　ruler
　　　　　1 sheet of copy paper
　　　　　15 or more pencils

Procedure

1. Lay the books on a table so that they are 6 inches (15 cm) apart.

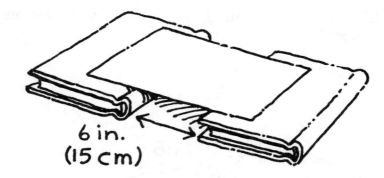

6 in.
(15 cm)

2. Use the sheet of paper to make a bridge between the two books. Make sure that an equal amount of the paper lies on each book.

3. Test the strength of the paper bridge by gently placing one pencil at a time in the center of the paper (between the books) until the paper falls.

4. Remove the paper from the books and fold it in half by placing the short ends together. Fold the paper again in the same direction.

5. Unfold the paper, then bend it accordion style to form an M shape.

6. Use the folded paper to form a bridge between the books as shown. Again, make sure that an equal amount of the paper is on each book.

7. Test the strength of the paper bridge by gently placing one pencil at a time across the top of the folded paper. If the pencil(s) tends to roll, use your finger to stop it. Count the pencils that the paper will support before falling.

8. Remove the M-shaped bridge and press its sides together. Then fold the paper in half, placing the long sides together.

9. Unfold the paper and bend it accordion style as before. The paper now has a double-M shape.

10. Place the paper bridge across the books.

11. Repeat step 7 with the double-M bridge.

Results The unfolded paper will not support even one pencil. Depending on the weight of the pencils, the M-shaped bridge may hold 4 to 6 pencils. The double-M bridge will hold more than twice as many pencils as the single-M bridge.

Why? A flat piece of paper is not very strong, but when it is folded in an accordion shape, it becomes stronger and can support more weight. This is because all of the object's weight pushes down on one part of the flat paper. But on the folded paper, the object's weight is spread out and smaller forces push down on different parts of the paper. The more folds, the more spread out the weight. For example, **corrugated** cardboard, which has a layer of grooves and ridges, is much stronger than flat cardboard.

Solutions to Exercises

1. *Think!*

- Floors are part of a structure, so they are permanent forces (dead forces).

- Windows are part of a structure, so they are permanent forces (dead forces).

- A desk is not part of a structure, since it can be removed easily, so it is a temporary force—that is, a live force.

Choice C is a live force.

2. *Think!*

- A lateral force pushes or pulls on the side of a structure.

- Force A shows snow on the roof. Snow adds weight to the house, so it is a gravitational force.

- Force B shows a window in the house. Windows add weight to the house, so force B is a gravitational force.

- Force C shows wind hitting against the side of the house.

Force C represents a lateral force.

2
Blast Off
Aerospace Engineering

What You Need to Know

Aerospace engineering is the branch of engineering concerned with the design, manufacture, and operation of launch vehicles, satellites, spacecraft, and ground-support facilities for the exploration of outer space. One type of spacecraft is a **rocket**, which is powered by gases that are forced out of one end. Rocket-like devices were demonstrated about 360 B.C. by the Greek mathematician and scientist Archytas (428–350 B.C.). So while some form of a rocket has been in existence for many years, the science of how a rocket works was first described by the British scientist Sir Isaac Newton (1642–1727) in 1687. Newton stated three important scientific principles that govern the motion of all objects, whether on Earth or in space. These principles, now called Newton's laws of motion, provided engineers with the basic knowledge necessary to design modern rockets such as the Saturn V rockets and the Space Shuttle *Discovery*.

Newton's first law of motion is a law about **inertia**, which is the tendency of an object at rest to remain at rest and an object in motion to remain in motion. An unbalanced force is needed to change the motion of an object; that is, the force starts or stops the motion of an object. When two or more forces act on an object, if the forces are equal and in opposite directions, the difference between the value of the forces is zero; thus, they are **balanced** and there is no motion. But if the forces are not equal in value, the difference between their value produces an **unbalanced force** (sum of unequal forces acting on an object). For example, if two boys are pulling on the ends of a rope in opposite directions and if one boy pulls with more force to the left, the resulting unbalanced force makes the rope and the boy holding the right end move to the left.

Newton's second law of motion explains how the force needed to **accelerate** (speed up) an object depends on the mass of the object. It takes more force to accelerate a car the same distance as a baseball because the car has a greater mass than the baseball. The same is true of **deceleration**, which means to slow down.

Newton's third law of motion explains that forces act in pairs. This law states that for every action there is an equal and opposite reaction. Newton realized that if one object applies a force on another, the second object applies an equal force on the first object but in the opposite direction. Each force in an action-reaction pair of forces is equal and acts in the opposite direction. But each force in the pair acts on a different object, so they are unbalanced forces. The action-reaction pairs in the diagram of the closed balloon are A_1/B_1 and A_2/B_2. You can be sure that two forces are action-reaction pairs if the objects in the description of one force can be interchanged to describe the other force. For example, "The gas inside the balloon pushes (force A) on the wall of the balloon. The wall of the balloon pushes (force B) on the gas inside."

In the figure of the open balloon, only one pair of the identified action-reaction forces is present: $A1/B1$. With the balloon open, the force of the gas and the force of the balloon are unbalanced forces. So the gas does **work** (applies a force over a distance) on the balloon, causing it to move up. The work done by the gas on the balloon is equal to the **energy** (ability to do work) of the gas pushing on it. Energy of moving objects

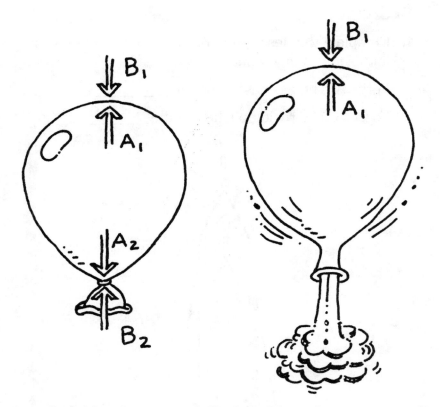

is called **kinetic energy**. Both work and energy equals
the product of a force times the distance the force is applied.
The energy and work of the gas on the balloon is equal to the
energy and work done by the balloon on the gas. This work
causes the gas to move down and out of the opening. With the
balloon closed, neither the force of the gas nor the force of the
balloon do work, meaning they don't cause anything to move.
This is because all the forces are balanced. Even so, the gas
and the balloon have **potential energy** (stored energy).

The same kinds of unbalanced forces make a rocket ship
move. The gas inside the rocket pushes up on the rocket, and
the rocket pushes the gas down and out. Aerospace engineers
must consider the best size and shape to use in designing
rockets that will produce just the right unbalanced forces.

Exercises

1. Complete the description of the action-reaction pair of forces for the diagram.

    Force A: The gas pushes on the _____.

    Force B: The rocket pushes on the _____.

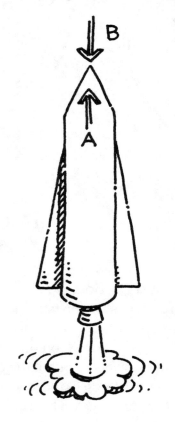

Legend	
Forces	**Description**
A	Gas inside rocket is acting on the rocket
B	Rocket is acting on gas inside the rocket.

2. Which diagram of a rocket, A or B, shows balanced forces?

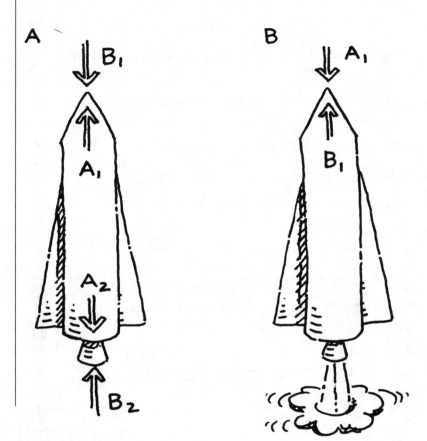

Activity: UNBALANCED

Purpose   To demonstrate the forces that propel a rocket.

Materials   6 feet (1.8 m) of string
4-inch (10-cm) piece of drinking straw
2 chairs
9-inch (23-cm) round balloon
spring clothespin
transparent tape

Procedure

1. Thread the string through the straw.

2. Tie the ends of the string to the backs of the chairs.

3. Position the chairs so that the string between them is as tight as possible.

4. Inflate the balloon. Twist the open end of the balloon and secure it with the clothespin.

5. Move the straw to one end of the string.

6. Tape the inflated balloon to the straw.

7. Remove the clothespin from the balloon.

Results The straw with the attached balloon quickly moves across the string. The movement stops at the end of the string or when the forces acting on the balloon are balanced.

Why? When the inflated balloon is closed, the air inside pushes equally in all directions. The balloon doesn't move because all the forces are balanced. When the balloon is open, the action-reaction pair of forces opposite the balloon's opening is unbalanced. One force is the walls of the balloon pushing on the gas inside the balloon. This force pushes the gas out of the balloon's opening. The other force is the gas pushing on the balloon's wall opposite the opening. This force pushes the balloon in the direction opposite the opening.

Solutions to Exercises

1. *Think!*

- Newton's third law of motion states that for every action there is an equal and opposite reaction; thus, if one object applies a force on another, the second object applies the same force on the first object.

- Action-reaction pairs of forces do not act on the same object.

- The objects in the description of one force in a pair of action-reaction forces can be interchanged to describe the other force.

Force A: The gas pushes on the rocket.

Force B: The rocket pushes on the gas.

2. *Think!*

- Forces A_1 and A_2 are equal in opposite directions and act on the rocket.

- Forces B_1 and B_2 are equal in opposite directions and act on the gas inside the rocket.

- Pairs of equal forces acting in opposite directions on the same object are balanced forces.

Figure A has two pairs of balanced forces.

3
Up and Away
Aeronautical Engineering

What You Need to Know

Aeronautical engineering is the branch of engineering concerned with the design, construction, and operation of aircraft. These engineers must have an understanding of **aerodynamics**, which is the study of the forces on an object due to the motion of the object through a **fluid** (gas or liquid) as well as the motion of the fluid on the object.

Air is the gas mixture in the **atmosphere** (layer of gas surrounding Earth). Examples of the aerodynamics of air include the study of the forces of **wind** (moving air) on a building and the study of the forces of air on **aircraft** (vehicles that can move through the air).

There are four basic forces that affect the **flight** (action of an object moving through the air) of an object through air: gravity, lift, thrust, and drag. The diagram shows how these forces are related for a straight, level flight. Gravity is the vertical downward force on an aircraft toward Earth's surface. Weight is the measure of the force of gravity. The greater the mass of the aircraft, the greater its weight, thus the greater the force of gravity on it. **Lift** is the vertical upward force on an aircraft. Weight and lift are forces in opposite directions. So for an aircraft to float in air, its lift force must be greater than its gravity force. **Thrust** is the forward force on an aircraft, and **drag** is the force in a direction opposite of thrust. Drag is an example of **friction**, which is any force that resists the motion between objects in contact with each other. For an aircraft to move forward, its thrust force must be greater than its drag force.

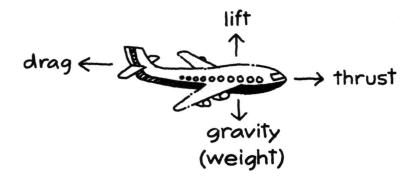

An airplane has lift because of the way air flows around the wings. Lift occurs if air moving over the top of the wing is faster than air moving over the bottom part of the wing. This is because as the speed of the air increases, the pressure it exerts on the surfaces it passes over decreases. This is known as **Bernoulli's principle.** So the slower-moving air under the wing applies more pressure on the wing than the faster-moving air flowing across the top of the wing. The lift under the wing has to be great enough to overcome the downward force of gravity as well as the downward force of air pressure on the top of the wing.

There are two ways to produce a difference in airspeed around an aircraft wing. One way is for the wing to be an **airfoil**, which is a surface designed to produce lift from air flowing around it. A curved upper surface of the wing creates less friction on the air flowing over it than does the flatter lower surface. The curved upper area makes the air above the wing travel a greater distance than the air beneath the wing. Because the air flowing over the top moves at a faster speed than air below the wing, the airstreams meet at the same time behind the wing. Lift occurs because the slower-moving air below the wing pushes up more than the faster-moving air above the wing pushes down. Another way to produce a difference in airspeed is to use a flat wing such as a kite and fly it at an angle to the wind. Air moves more quickly over the top of the slanted wing, again creating lift.

Exercises

1. The figure shows the side view of an airplane wing. Using the words "higher" and "lower," fill in the blanks below for each part described.

   a. Because the upper surface of the wing is more curved than its underside, in comparison to the airspeed below the wing, the air moving over the top has a _____ airspeed.

   b. Because the lower surface of the wing is flatter than the upper surface, in comparison to the airspeed above the wing, the air moving over the bottom of the wing has a _____ airspeed.

   c. The difference between airspeed over the top and bottom of the wing creates an area of _____ pressure above the wing and _____ pressure below the wing.

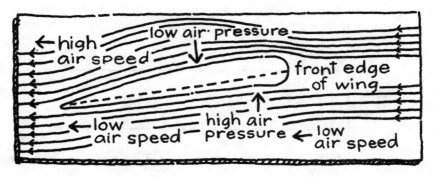

2. The difference between the air pressure above and below an airplane creates the force called _____.

Activity: LIFTER

Purpose   To demonstrate the forces acting on a wing.

Materials   scissors
ruler
file folder
pencil
paper hole punch
transparent tape
lemon-sized piece of modeling clay
12-inch (30-cm) wooden skewer
handheld hair dryer
adult helper

Procedure

1. Cut a paper strip measuring 2-by-11-inches (5-by-27.5 cm) from the file folder.

2. Draw three lines across the paper strip, at 1/2 inch (1.25 cm), 4 inches (10 cm), and 7 inches (17.5 cm) from one end. Label the lines A, B, and C.

3. Using the paper hole punch, cut a hole in the center of lines B and C.

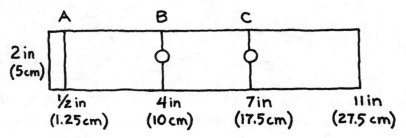

4. Bend the end closest to line C back so that the end touches line A. Do not crease the bend. Secure the teardrop-shaped loop with a piece of tape.

5. Place a grape-sized piece of clay on the pointed end of the wooded skewer. Stand the remaining clay on a table.

6. Push the free, flat end of the wooden skewer through the holes in the paper and into the clay. Position the skewer so that it stands vertically.

7. With adult supervision, set the hair dryer on the cool setting at high speed. Hold the hair dryer about 6 inches (15 cm) in front of the rounded side of the paper so that more of the air flows over the upper part of the wing. Adjust the position of the hair dryer so that the paper lifts.

Results The paper lifts as air passes around the wing.

Why? The paper wing is an example of an airfoil. Directing the air so that more flows over the upper surface creates lower pressure above the wing than below it. The air hitting the front of the airfoil splits. The part of the air flowing over the more curved upper surface has less friction, thus a faster speed and less pressure on the wing than the air flowing over the less curved lower section of the wing. The difference between the air pressure creates lift on the wing, causing it to rise on the wooden skewer.

Solutions to Exercises

1a. *Think!*

- The curved upper section has less friction than the air beneath the wing. This causes the air above the wing to move faster, creating a lower pressure than the air beneath the wing.

In comparison to the airspeed below the wing, the air moving over the top of the wing has a high airspeed.

1b. *Think!*

- The bottom of the wing is less curved than the top; thus, it has more friction.

- An increase in friction causes a decrease in speed.

In comparison to the airspeed above the wing, the air moving over the bottom of the wing has a low airspeed.

1c. *Think!*

- According to Bernoulli's principle, as the speed of the air increases over a surface, the air pressure on that surface decreases.

- The speed of the air is greater above the wing than below it.

- The speed of the air is less below the wing than above it.

The difference between the airspeed over the top and bottom of the wing creates an area of low pressure above the wing and high pressure below the wing.

2. **Think!**

- The pressure below the wing is greater than above the wing.

- The greater pressure below the wing causes the wing to rise.

- What is the flight force that causes a wing to rise?

The difference between the air pressure above and below an airplane wing creates the force called lift.

4

Up and Down

Roller-Coaster Engineering

What You Need to Know

Roller-coaster engineering is the branch of engineering concerned with designing, constructing, and testing roller-coaster cars and the paths they follow. Since part of the testing means these engineers have to actually ride on the roller coasters, you might think this would be a pretty fun job. In designing roller coasters, engineers try to create a ride that is thrilling and fun but also safe.

When moving up hill on a roller-coaster track, the cars are moving against the pull of gravity. So the train of cars must be pulled up the first and generally the tallest hill of the track. At the top of the hill, the cars have potential energy (stored energy). The amount of potential energy of an object that is raised depends on its weight (force of gravity) and the height it is raised. The greater its weight and the higher it is raised, the greater the potential energy. Generally, the potential energy of the roller-coaster cars at the top of the first hill is their source of energy for the rest of the ride. This is because energy (ability to do work) can be changed from one form to another.

Kinetic energy is the energy of a moving object. As gravity pulls the cars down the first hill, their potential energy begins to change to kinetic energy. The farther they move, the faster they move and the more kinetic energy they have. They reach their fastest speed at the bottom of the hill. At this point, they have zero potential energy and maximum kinetic energy. The cars continue to move, climbing the second hill using kinetic energy. As they move up the hill, they are again moving against the pull of gravity, which decreases their speed and kinetic energy. However, their potential energy increases again as their height increases.

At the top of the second hill, the cars have zero kinetic energy and maximum potential energy. But the amount of potential energy is less than the original amount. This is because some of the original potential energy was changed into other forms of energy such as heat and sound that do not cause the cars to move. As the total potential energy decreases, the total kinetic energy also decreases. As the kinetic energy decreases, the hills must be shorter.

Some roller coasters include loops. Roller-coaster engineers have to design the loops so that the cars can stay on the track even when they are upside down. For the cars to move in a circular path, there must be a constant force pushing them toward the center of the curved path. This center-seeking force is called **centripetal force**. This action force is balanced by a center-fleeing reaction force called **centrifugal force**. While centripetal force is a real force acting on the moving cars, centrifugal force is an apparent force due to inertia.

Inertia is the tendency of an object at rest to remain at rest and for an object in motion to continue in motion. If an object is going in a straight line, it tends to keep going in a straight line. This is what happens to a roller-coaster car. As the car goes up into the loop, the car keeps going in a straight line but the track pushes it toward the center of the loop. Inertia creates what seems like a force pushing the car outward from the cen-

ter of the looped track. It is not a real force; instead, it is inertia trying to make the car go in a straight line. The faster the
car moves, the greater its centripetal and centrifugal forces.

The speed necessary to hold the car on the track depends on
the shape of the loop. Roller-coaster engineers want a loop
that makes the ride exciting, but it also has to be safe. If the
loop were a perfect circle, the speed needed to keep the car
on the track would create a force that would be harmful to the
people riding the roller coaster.

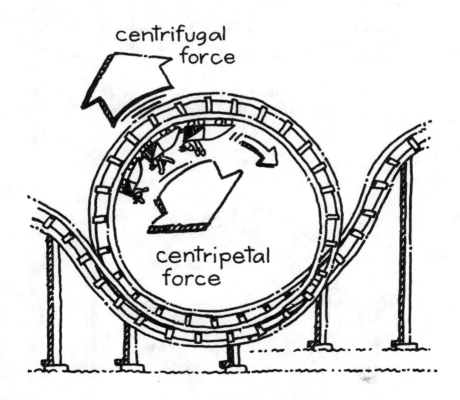

Exercises

1. In the diagram, in which position, A or B, do the cars of the roller coaster have the most potential energy?

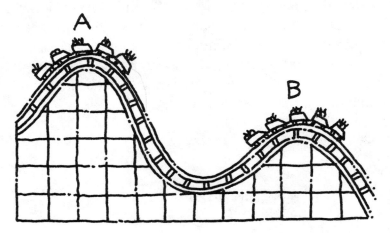

2. In the diagram, which arrow, A, B, C, or D, represents a centripetal force on the roller-coaster car?

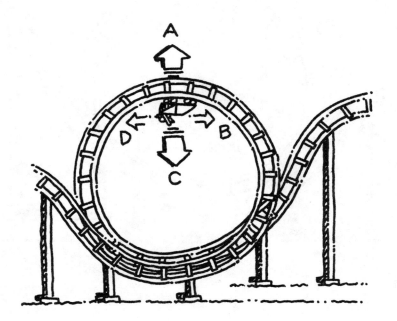

Activity: AROUND AND AROUND

Purpose To demonstrate how a roller coaster moves around a loop.

Materials pencil
ruler
10-by-28-inch (25-by-40-cm) piece of poster board
scissors
transparent tape
marble
helper

Procedure

1. Draw a 2-by-6-inch (5-by-15-cm) rectangle in the center of one end of the poster board. Cut out the rectangle to create two tabs on the end of the poster board. Label the tabs A and B as shown.

2. On both sides of the poster board, make a mark 15 inches (37.5 cm) from the uncut end. Label the marks A and B as shown.

3. Bend about half of both tabs. Then bend the poster board over in a loop so that tab A touches mark A, and tab B touches mark B. Tape the tabs to the marks.

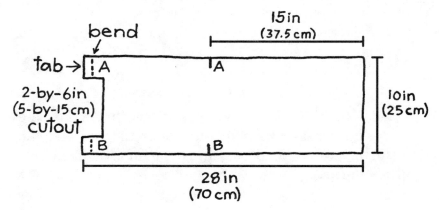

4. Tape the free end of the poster board to the edge of a cabinet and then pull the board away from the cabinet so that the paper is at a slight angle from vertical (straight up and down).

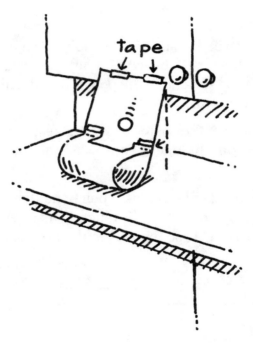

5. Stand to the side so that you can see inside the loop of the poster board and ask a helper to release the marble at the top of the poster board. Observe the motion of the marble inside the loop.

Results The marble rolls around the loop one or more times.

Why? Raising the marble to the top of the paper gives it potential energy. When the marble is released, its potential energy changes into kinetic energy. If the marble has enough kinetic energy, it will move around the loop. When the moving marble goes into the loop, it turns upward. If the marble has enough kinetic energy to raise it to the top of the loop, then gravity pulls it down the other side. The centripetal force and centrifugal force keep the marble on the paper loop. As the marble moves, the friction (force that resists the motion of objects in contact with each other) between the paper and the marble causes the marble to lose energy until finally it does not have enough energy to rise to the top of the loop.

Solutions to Exercises

1. *Think!*

   - Potential energy is the stored energy an object has due to position or condition.

   - The higher an object is raised, the more potential energy it has.

   - The cars on the highest hill have the most potential energy.

   Cars on hill A have the most potential energy.

2. *Think!*

   - Centripetal force is a force on an object moving in a circular path.

   - Centripetal force is directed inward toward the center of the circular path.

   Arrow C represents centripetal force.

5
Coming Through
Solar Engineering

What You Need to Know

Solar engineering is the branch of engineering concerned with designing structures and processes to capture and use solar energy. **Solar energy** is radiant energy from the Sun. **Radiant energy**, also called **radiation**, is energy traveling in the form of waves called **electromagnetic waves** that can move through space. All other forms of energy can only move through materials. Radiation is also the name of the method by which radiant energy travels.

Radiant energy comes in different forms depending on the energy of its electromagnetic waves. All the types of radiant energy listed in order of their energy level make up the **electromagnetic spectrum**. The solar energy leaving the Sun contains every type of radiant energy. But when this mixture of radiant energy enters Earth's atmosphere, some is **reflected** (bounced back from a surface) back into space, some is **absorbed** (taken in) by the different gases in the air, and some passes through to Earth's surface. The radiation reaching Earth's surface is mainly infrared radiation, ultraviolet radiation, and visible light, with most being visible light. **Infrared radiation (IR)** is invisible radiant energy that your skin senses as heat, so it is often called heat waves. **Ultraviolet radiation (UV)** is invisible radiant energy that can cause your skin to tan, but in excess it can damage your skin.

Visible light is the only type of radiant energy that the human eye can see. The different types of visible light listed in order of their energy levels make up the visible spectrum. The colors in the **visible spectrum** listed from least to greatest energy are red, orange, yellow, green, blue, indigo, and violet.

Whether radiant energy is absorbed, reflected, and/or passes through a material depends on whether the material is transparent, translucent, or opaque. If you can see through a material, it is **transparent** to visible light, which means it allows visible light to easily pass through—for example, glass. A material that allows radiant energy to pass through but scatters it in different directions is **translucent** to that form of radiant energy. For example, frosted glass is translucent to visible light. This is why things viewed through frosted glass look blurred. If a type of radiant energy cannot pass through a material, the material is **opaque** to that type of radiant energy. For example, you cannot see through this book, so it is opaque to visible light. Things that are transparent to one type of radiant energy can be opaque to another type. For example, glass is transparent to visible light and ultraviolet radiation but is opaque to infrared radiation.

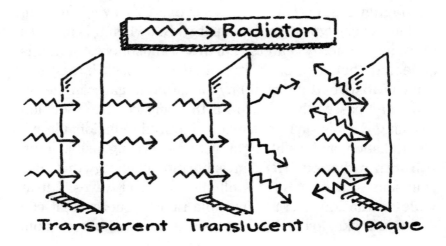

Transparent   Translucent   Opaque

Unless stated otherwise, the terms *transparent, translucent,* and *opaque* refer to visible light. Opaque materials absorb and/or reflect radiant energy depending on the surface and makeup of the material. Materials with dark, dull, and rough surfaces absorb more energy, and materials with light, shiny, and smooth surfaces reflect more energy.

Solar energy passing through a window of clear glass is mostly visible light. Visible light that is absorbed by a material causes the particles in the material to move faster, thus increasing its temperature. Solar engineers use the knowledge of how materials react to solar radiation in designing structures that can capture and use solar energy for heating.

Exercises

1. Which glass jar diagram, A, B, or C, represents the fact that glass is transparent to visible light but opaque to infrared radiation?

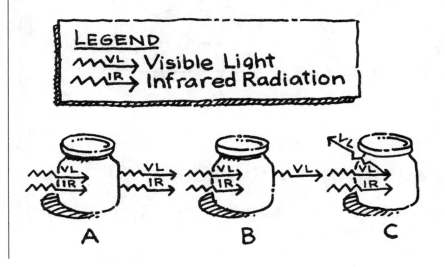

2. Study the diagram and determine which arrow, A, B, or C, represents the radiation (infrared radiation, ultraviolet radiation, and visible light) to which Earth's atmosphere is the most transparent.

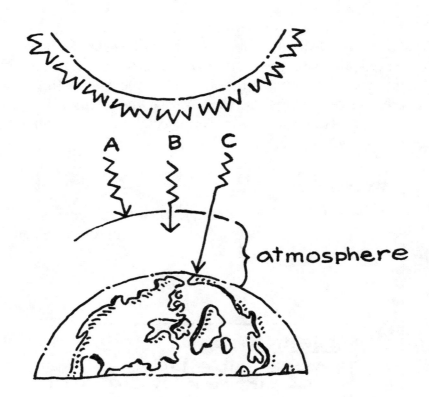

Activity: PASSING THROUGH

Purpose To demonstrate that visible light from the Sun can heat materials.

Materials 1-cup (250-mL) measuring cup
cold tap water
2 identical quart (liter) glass jars with lids
2 tea bags
aluminum foil

Procedure

1. Pour 1 cup (250 mL) of cold water into each of the jars.

2. Place one tea bag in each jar. Close each jar with a lid.

3. Wrap one of the jars with aluminum foil, leaving only the lid exposed.

4. Place both jars outdoors in direct sunlight.

5. After 15 minutes, gently shake each jar to mix the contents.

6. Remove the lids from each jar and the aluminum foil. Then compare the color of the liquid in each jar.

Results The color of the water in the jar covered with aluminum foil is a pale brown. The color of the water in the uncovered jar is much darker.

Why? Tea bags contain small pieces of tea leaves, which contain brown particles that dissolve more quickly in warm water than in cold. The more tea particles dissolved in the water, the darker the mixture. The glass is opaque to infrared radiation (heat waves) but is transparent to visible light. So the water absorbs the visible light passing through the glass, causing it to heat up. The warmer the water, the faster the tea particles dissolve. The aluminum foil is opaque to visible light, so none enters the covered jar. In the cooler water in the covered jar, the tea particles dissolve slowly. Since there are fewer colored tea particles, the mixture has a pale color.

Solutions to Exercises

1. *Think!*

    - Visible light can pass through a glass jar.

    - Infrared radiation is absorbed by glass; thus, it does not pass through the glass.

    Diagram B represents glass that is transparent to visible light but opaque to infrared radiation.

2. *Think!*

    - Transparent means to pass through.

- The arrow passing through Earth's atmosphere represents the radiation to which the atmosphere is most transparent.

Arrow C represents the radiation to which Earth's atmosphere is the most transparent.

6

Easy Listening

Acoustical Engineering

What You Need to Know

Acoustical engineering is the branch of engineering dealing with **acoustics**, which is how sound behaves in and is affected by a structure. With their knowledge of sound, including how it is produced and how to increase or decrease its loudness, acoustical engineers design and assist in the building of structures with specific acoustics. For example, the acoustics for a hospital, where people expect quiet, is different from the acoustics needed for a sports arena or a concert hall.

Acoustical engineers are sound experts. **Sound** is a type of energy. It is a wave created by and transferred by **vibrating** (back-and-forth or to-and-fro motion) materials such as air. **Sound waves** in air enter your ears. Then your ears send signals to your brain that interprets the quality of the sound. Materials vibrating at different speeds send out different-size sound waves that the brain interprets as having different qualities, such as being high, low, loud, or soft.

If sounds are easily heard in a room, it is said to have good acoustics. The acoustics of a room depend on how sound waves behave when they hit objects in the room. Three things can happen depending on the type of surface the sound waves hit: (1) Sound waves reflect (bounce) off of hard and slick materials such as mirrors, wooden floors, and furniture.

(2) Sound waves are absorbed (taken in) by soft, fuzzy materials such as carpet, curtains, and padded furniture and by rough materials such as textured walls. Sound gets trapped in these materials because most of it bounces around in the material instead of being reflected. The trapped sound energy changes to heat energy. (3) Sound waves are **diffused** (scattered in many different directions) by objects with hard and smooth but uneven surfaces such as books of different sizes on a shelf. This is because some of the sound waves bounce between the surfaces before being reflected.

Reflection   Absorption

Diffusion

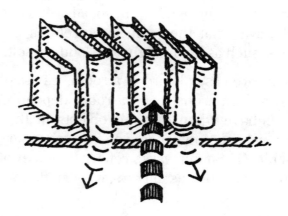

If you walk into a room filled with cloth-covered furniture, carpeting on the floor, and curtains on the windows, you may not hear the sound made by your steps. But if the same room were empty of furniture, carpet, and curtains, the sound made by your steps would be much louder. This is because the furnishings, curtains, and carpet absorb the sound, whereas the walls and floor of the empty room reflect the sound. **Echos** are reflected sound waves. In the empty room, you hear the original sound produced by your steps plus all the echos of the reflected sound waves.

Exercises

1. Put your hand over the front of your throat, close your mouth, and hum. Then pinch your nose closed with your fingers and try to hum. Which statement is true?

    a. With your nose open, you felt movement in your throat as you hummed.

    b. With your nose closed, you heard a sound.

2. Which of the toys, A, B, or C, absorbs the most sound?

A

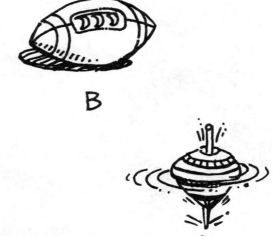

B

C

Activity: QUIET PLEASE

Purpose To determine how to make a room quieter.

Materials ticking timer
shoe box
2 pencils
cotton balls (enough to fill the shoe box)

Procedure

1. Make sure that any background sounds are at a minimum. (Turn off the TV or stereo, for example.)

2. At the end of a large room or hallway, turn the timer on and place it in the shoe box. Place the lid on the box and set the box on a table or the floor.

3. Walk in a straight line away from the box until you no longer hear the ticking.

4. Place a pencil on the floor to mark this spot.

5. Fill the box with the cotton balls. Stuff the cotton under and over the timer, but keep the timer pointed in the same direction within the box.

6. With the box in the same place as before, again walk away from it until you no longer hear the ticking. (Make sure the background sounds are the same as before.)

7. Mark the distance with the second pencil. Which pencil is closer to the box?

Results The pencil marking the distance from the cotton-filled box should be closer to the box.

Why? Insulation is any material through which energy is poorly transferred. Since sound is a type of energy and cotton is a good insulator, the cotton absorbs much of the sound and keeps it from being transferred out of the box; that is, the cotton muffles the sound. Loudness depends on the energy of the sound. Since the ticking of the clock in the cotton-filled box can be heard only when you're close to the box, this means that the energy of the sound leaving the cotton-filled box is less than the energy of the sound leaving the box with no insulation.

Solutions to Exercises

1. *Think!*

   • Sound is produced when something vibrates.

   • Humming is produced when air from your lungs moves through your voice box, causing it to vibrate.

   • When your voice box vibrates, your throat vibrates.

- When you stop the airflow by pinching your nose, your voice box does not vibrate, so you can't make much of a sound.

Statement a is true.

2. ***Think!***

- Sound that hits fuzzy material gets trapped because the sound bounces around in the material instead of being reflected.

- Which of the toys has the fuzziest surface?

Toy A, the bear, absorbs more sound than the other toys.

7
Stop and Go
Electrical Engineering

What You Need to Know

Electrical engineering is the branch of engineering concerned with designing things and systems that use electricity. **Electricity** is a form of energy produced by the presence or movement of electrical charges. An **electric charge** is the property of particles that causes a force between them. There are two types of charges: positive and negative. The center of an **atom** (the basic building block of all substances) is called the **nucleus**. **Protons** are positively charged particles inside an atom's nucleus, and **electrons** are negatively charged particles outside the nucleus.

There are two kinds of electricity: static and current. **Static electricity** comes from a buildup of stationary charges. Uncharged atoms in all materials have an equal number of positive and negative charges. Electrons can be transferred from one material to another, so a material becomes positively charged when its atoms lose electrons and negatively charged when its atoms gain electrons. When two like charges (positive and positive or negative and negative) are near each other, they **repel** (push apart) each other. So electrons repel electrons, and protons repel protons. When two unlike charges (positive and negative) are near each other, they **attract** (pull together) each other. So electrons and protons attract each other.

Static discharge is the loss of static electricity that occurs when electrons are transferred to another material. **Lightning** is a high-energy, visible static discharge between clouds and other objects such as Earth, buildings, or people. Other less energetic discharges occur in machines, which can be damaging to sensitive parts and can cost a great deal of money. Electrical engineers design ways to prevent static discharge or to protect machinery from its effects. These designs include the use of insulation, which are materials that inhibit the transfer of energy, including electricity. For example, electrical engineers avoid using wood, cloth, and paper as insulators because on very humid days these insulating materials absorb water and can **conduct** (transfer) electricity. Instead, they use plastics and rubber, which are good insulators that do not tend to absorb water.

Current electricity is due to the motion of **free electrons** (electrons that are not tightly bound to a single atom and are relatively free to move from one atom to another). **Electric conduction** is the transfer of electricity due to the movement of free electrons in a material. Materials that easily conduct electricity have many free electrons and are called **electric conductors**. **Metals**, which are elements that are usually shiny solids such as silver, gold, and copper, are good conductors, especially silver, copper, and aluminum. Metals are used to create **electric circuits**, which are pathways for electricity. Electricity will not flow unless the circuit is complete. The diagram shows an open circuit and a closed circuit. The **battery** is a device that changes chemical energy into electric energy. The battery causes the charges to move through a circuit. In the **open circuit** there is a break in the path, so no electricity flows through the light and it does not glow. In the **closed circuit** there are no breaks in the path, so the bulb glows.

Materials with poor electric conduction, such as rubber, glass, dry wood, plastic, and air, are called insulators. Insulators are poor conductors of any type of energy. An insulator, unlike a conductor, is more easily charged with static electricity, since charges do not easily move through it.

Open Circuit

Closed Circuit

Exercises

1. A balloon is rubbed with a cloth, causing the balloon to be negatively charged. Which diagram, A or B, represents the change from a neutral to a negatively charged balloon?

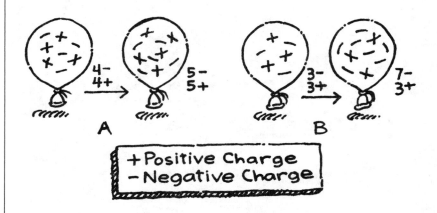

2. Which diagram, A or B, is a closed circuit?

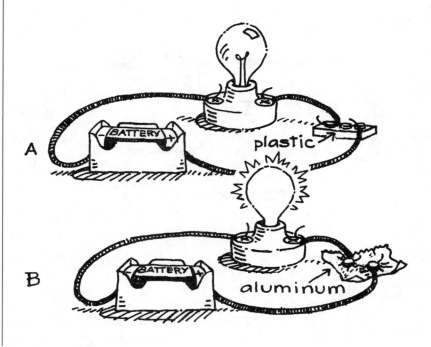

Activity: PASSING THROUGH

Purpose To determine if a material is a conductor or an insulator for electric energy.

Materials flashlight with 2 D-cell batteries
1-by-4-inch piece of copy paper
transparent tape
1-by-4-inch piece of aluminum foil

Procedure

1. Turn the flashlight on to make sure that it works properly, then turn it off.

2. Open the flashlight and remove one of the batteries.

3. Tape the copy paper strip over the positive end of the battery as shown.

4. Place the paper-covered battery back in the flashlight and close the flashlight. Turn the light on and observe whether the light glows.

5. Open the flashlight and remove the paper-covered battery. Remove the paper and replace it with the strip of aluminum foil.

6. Place the aluminum-covered battery back in the flashlight and close the flashlight. Turn the light on and observe whether the light glows.

Results The flashlight bulb glows when the battery is covered with aluminum foil, but it doesn't glow when the battery is covered with paper.

Why? Aluminum foil is a conductor and paper is an insulator. When the aluminum covers the battery, electricity is able to flow from the battery through the aluminum to the bulb, so the bulb glows. The aluminum foil completes the circuit. But the paper breaks the circuit because electricity cannot flow through it. The bulb does not glow when the paper covers the battery.

Solutions for Exercises

1. *Think!*

   • A negatively charged balloon has more negative charges than positive charges.

   • The second balloon in diagram B has seven negative charges and three positive charges.

   Diagram B represents the change from a neutral to a negatively charged balloon.

2. *Think!*

   • In diagram A, the wires leading to the lightbulb are broken and connected to a piece of plastic, which is an insulator. An insulator does not allow electricity to flow through it.

- In diagram B, the wires are connected to a piece of aluminum, which is a good conductor. A conductor allows electricity to flow through it.

- Electricity can flow through a closed circuit.

- The bulb glows when the circuit is closed.

Diagram B is a closed circuit.

8

Directors

Optical Engineering

What You Need to Know

Optical engineering is the branch of engineering concerned with designing, constructing, and testing optical instruments. **Optical** refers to sight or light. An **optical instrument** is any device that directs the path of light in order to better assist sight. Optical instruments include eyeglasses, microscopes, telescopes, and binoculars. **Eyeglasses** allow a person to clearly see objects at distances that appear blurry without them. **Microscopes** assist in studying things too small for the unaided eye to see clearly. **Telescopes** and **binoculars** assist the eye in seeing distant objects.

Optical instruments contain lenses and/or mirrors that change the direction of light entering and leaving them. A **lens** is a shaped piece of transparent material, such as glass or plastic. The shape of a transparent material changes the direction of the path of light passing through it. If the lens has two curved sides, it is called a double lens. If it has one curved side, it is called a single lens. A **convex lens** has a surface that curves outward like the surface of a ball. This lens is thicker in the center than at the edges. A magnifying lens is an example of a double convex lens. The line passing through the center of any lens or curved mirror is called the **principal axis**. Any convex lens, single or double, causes light rays parallel to its principal axis to **converge** toward the axis. This means they pass through the lens and bend toward and meet at a single point, called the **focal point,** on the principal axis. A concave lens has a surface that is curved inward like the bowl of a spoon. This lens causes light rays passing through it parallel to its principal axis to **diverge,** meaning that light rays bend away from the principal axis.

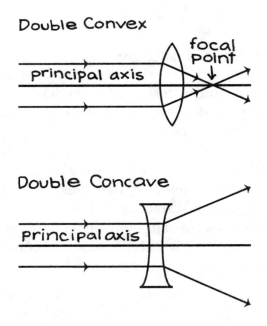

A **mirror** has a surface that reflects (bounces back from a surface) light. If a mirror is flat, light will be reflected at the same angle that it hits the mirror's surface as shown in the diagram where angle A equals angle B. The surface of a concave mirror curves inward. If the light rays hitting a concave mirror are parallel to the principal axis, they will be reflected toward the focal point. This means that these reflected rays converge at the focal point in front of the mirror. Convex mirrors have a surface that curves outward. This surface causes light rays parallel to the principal axis to be reflected away from the principal axis—that is, to diverge.

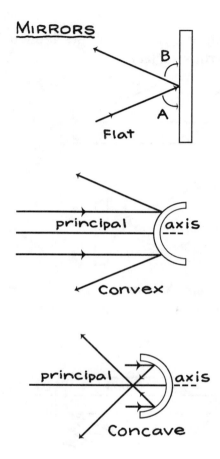

Mirrors and lenses are used in optical equipment such as microscopes and telescopes. Refracting telescopes use only lenses while reflecting telescopes use both mirrors and lenses. Lenses or a combination of lenses and mirrors help your eyes gather more light so that you see distant objects better through a telescope. Because of the way lenses or the combination of lenses and mirrors in most telescopes bend light rays, the **images** (representations of physical objects formed by a lens or mirror) you see are upside down.

Exercises

1. Which diagram, A or B, shows light being reflected from a mirror's surface?

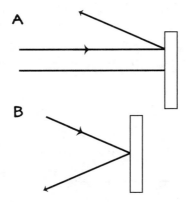

2. Which diagram, A, B, or C, represents light diverging as it reflects from a convex mirror?

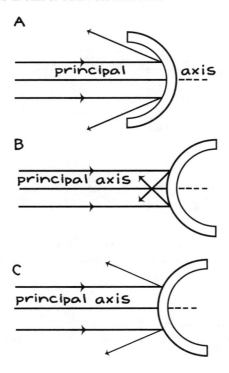

Activity: UP OR DOWN

Purpose   To determine the effect of the shape of a mirror on the image it produces.

Material   large metal spoon

Procedure

1. Hold the spoon with the inside of the bowl facing you.

2. Move the spoon back and forth from your face until the clearest image is formed. Observe whether the image is right side up or upside down.

3. Repeat steps 1 and 2, turning the spoon so that the bottom of it faces you.

Results   When you look into the inside of a spoon, your image is upside down. When you look into the outside of a spoon, your image is right side up.

Why?   The inside of the spoon has a concave surface. Light rays reflecting from the concave surface of the spoon's bowl converges in front of the spoon. These light rays form a small, upside-down image. When holding the concave side of the spoon close to your face, you see an upside-down image of your face as shown in the diagram. Light reflecting from a convex surface, such as the outside of a spoon's bowl, diverges. Even though it is not real, your brain sends a message that the rays converge behind the spoon. Thus you see a small right-side-up image as shown.

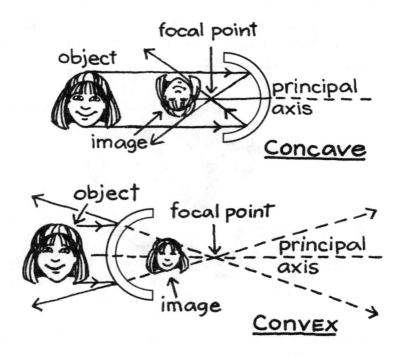

Solutions to Exercises

1. *Think!*

   • A mirror is a polished surface that reflects light.

   • When light bounces back from a surface, it is said to be reflected.

- Light reflects from a flat mirror at the same angle that it strikes the mirror's surface.

Diagram B shows light reflecting from a flat mirror.

2. **Think!**

- A convex mirror curves outward.

- A convex mirror cause light rays to diverge; that is, to spread away from the normal.

Diagram C represents a convex mirror that diverges reflected light rays.

9

Recover

Petroleum Engineering

What You Need to Know

Petroleum is a common name for crude oil and any of its products. **Crude oil** is a natural, **nonrenewable energy resource**, which is a source of energy that cannot be replaced and can be used up.

Most petroleum is used to make fuels such as diesel, gasoline, and aircraft fuel. Some petroleum is used to make heating oil, lubricants, and plastics. It is also used in other products such as aspirin, toothpaste, and detergents. The figure shows the percent of the U.S. petroleum supply used for different products.

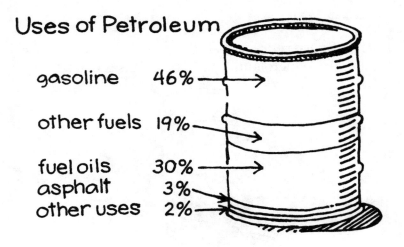

Uses of Petroleum

gasoline   46%

other fuels 19%

fuel oils   30%
asphalt   3%
other uses   2%

Petroleum engineering is the branch of engineering concerned with discovering underground regions containing crude oil as well as natural gas, which is another nonrenewable energy resource. Once these regions are found, petroleum engineers work with other specialists to determine how to remove the petroleum. They decide on drilling methods, which can involve designing and constructing equipment as well as processes that get as much petroleum as possible out of the ground.

Petroleum engineers may use water to cause the oil to float to the surface. This recovery method depends on two physical properties: miscibility and density. **Miscibility** describes a substance's ability to mix and thoroughly blend with another substance. Substances that are not able to mix and blend together are said to be **immiscible**. **Density** describes the mass of a certain volume of a substance. Density is used to determine the **buoyancy** (ability to float) of materials. Since oil and water are immiscible and oil has a lower density than water, oil is more buoyant than water. This means that when oil and water are mixed, oil floats on top of the water. As the water level rises, the oil is forced out of the ground.

Exercises

1. The figure represents the mixture of three immiscible liquids. Which liquid, A, B, or C, has the least density?

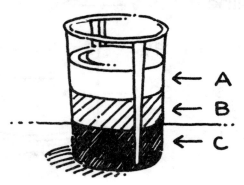

2. In the figure, water is being poured into a jar containing oil. After the mixture has had time to settle, which jar, A, B, or C, represents the results?

Activity: SEPARATE

Purpose   To demonstrate the difference in the densities of oil and water.

Materials   ½ cup (125 mL) cooking oil
empty 20-ounce (600 mL) plastic water bottle with cap
tap water
blue food coloring

Procedure

1. Pour the oil into the bottle.

2. Add water to the bottle until it is about half full. Notice that the water sinks and collects at the bottom of the bottle.

3. Add 5 or 6 drops of food coloring to the bottle.

4. Put the cap on the bottle, then vigorously shake the bottle.

5. Immediately observe the contents of the bottle, then observe the bottle periodically for 1 hour or longer. Then allow the bottle to sit undisturbed overnight.

Results After shaking the bottle, at first it appears that the contents have blended together. But in a short time, the contents divide into three layers. After 24 hours, there are only two layers.

Why? Shaking causes bubbles of oil and bubbles of water to form. Water has a higher density, so it sinks to the bottom, carrying with it trapped bubbles of oil. The center layer is mostly a mixture of oil and water bubbles. This layer is in the center because its density is greater than oil but less than water. Thus it is more buoyant than water but less buoyant than oil. The top layer is made mostly of oil, which has the least density. It rises, carrying with it trapped bubbles of water. After 24 hours, the oil and water separate into two layers: oil on top and water on bottom. The blue food coloring is water soluble, meaning it dissolves in water: thus, the bottom water layer is blue.

Solutions to Exercises

1. *Think!*

   - The liquids separate because they are immiscible, meaning they do not mix.

   - There are three separate layers because each layer has a different density.

   - The liquid with the least density has the greatest buoyancy, meaning it floats on the top.

   Liquid A has the least density.

2. *Think!*

   - Water and oil are immiscible, meaning they do not mix. Instead, they separate into layers.

- The density of water is greater than the density of oil.

- In immiscible mixtures of liquids, the less dense liquid floats on top of the liquid with the greater density.

Jar B represents the results of mixing water and oil.

10

Break Out

Nuclear Engineering

What You Need to Know

All atoms have a center part called the nucleus. The particles inside the nucleus are called **nucleons**. Nucleons that are positively charged are called protons, and nucleons with no charge are called **neutrons**. **Nuclear energy** is given off during a **nuclear reaction**, which occurs when there is any change in an atom's nucleus.

Nuclear engineering is the branch of engineering concerned with nuclear energy. Nuclear engineers design and develop processes, instruments, and systems so that nuclear energy can be used safely. Examples are **nuclear reactors** (devices that control nuclear reactions) and submarines powered by nuclear energy, as well as equipment such as special cameras used to map the movement of radioactive materials through a person's body in order to diagnose medical problems.

Elements are substances made of one kind of atom. The identity of an atom is determined by its **atomic number**, which is the number of protons in its nucleus. For example, the element uranium has an atomic number of 92, so each atom of uranium has 92 protons in its nucleus. The **atomic mass** of an atom is the sum of the total number of protons and neutrons in its nucleus. Atoms of the same element have the same atomic number, but they can differ in their atomic mass because they can have different numbers of neutrons. The mass number is sometimes part of an atom's name or symbol such as uranium-235 or U-235.

Nuclear fission is a type of nuclear reaction in which a large nucleus, such as that of a uranium atom, is bombarded by a fast-moving neutron. The result is that the nucleus splits into two roughly equal parts, which form two different types of atoms, releasing large amounts of energy and usually two or more fast-moving neutrons. The figure shows the nuclear fission of a uranium-235 atom, resulting in two smaller atoms, three neutrons, and lots of energy. Examples of fission products include barium (atomic number 56) and krypton (atomic number 36). Note that the atomic numbers add up to 92, which is the atomic number of uranium. This is because the protons in uranium split, forming two new types of atoms. But the sum of the atomic mass of the fission products equals 232 because three neutrons are released.

In a **nuclear reactor**, controlled nuclear fission reactions occur, and the released energy is used to heat water. The heat energy from the water is transferred to other devices that use it to produce electricity. The fission of uranium can produce a **chain reaction**, which is a nuclear reaction in which the material that starts the reaction is also one of the products. For example, a fast-moving neutron causes the fission of one uranium nucleus, resulting in the release of more fast-moving neutrons, which can cause the fission of other uranium nuclei, thus producing more fast-moving neutrons, and so on. In order to keep the nuclear reaction from getting out of control, nuclear engineers use **control rods** in nuclear reactors to absorb neutrons, thus reducing the number of neutrons available to strike uranium nuclei. These rods can be raised or lowered to control the amount of neutrons available. If the fission rate is too slow, the rods are raised. If the fission rate is too fast, the rods are lowered.

Exercises

1. Which diagram, A or B, represents a fission reaction?

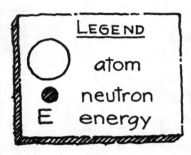

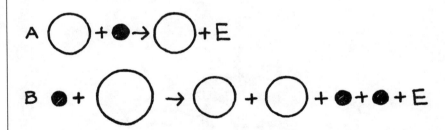

2. Which diagram on page 76, A or B, shows the slowing down of the fission reactions in a nuclear reactor?

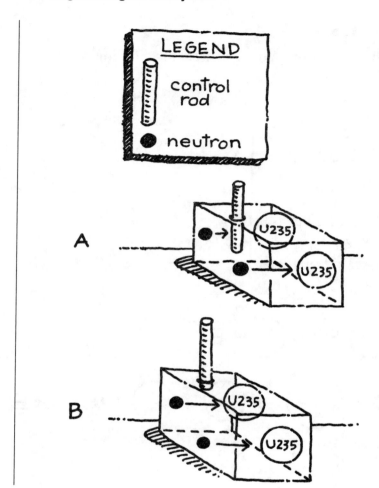

Activity: STICKERS

Purpose   To model how control rods in a nuclear reactor affect the fission rate.

Materials   2-inch (5-cm)-wide transparent tape
10–20 cotton balls
plastic container large enough to hold the cotton
balls

Procedure

1. Attach one end of the tape to the center and top of a door frame. Unwind enough tape for the strip to hang about 6 inches (15 cm) from the floor.

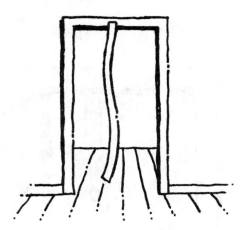

2. Put the cotton balls in the plastic container. The cotton balls represent neutrons.

3. Hold the container and stand about 3 feet (0.9 m) from the sticky side of the tape. The tape represents a control rod in a nuclear reactor.

4. Throw the cotton balls toward the tape. Count the number that stick to the tape. The cotton balls that do not stick to the tape represent neutrons that are not absorbed by control rods and are therefore available to hit the nuclei of atoms, causing fission reactions.

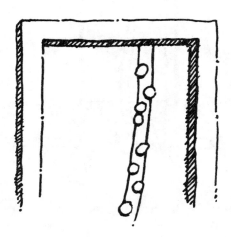

5. Repeat this activity using more strips of tape to demonstrate how the number of control rods affect the amount of neutrons available for fission reactions.

Results Some of the cotton balls hit and stick to the tape, while others pass through the open door. The more pieces of tape, the greater the number of cotton balls that stick to the tape and the fewer that pass through the door.

Why? Control rods are made of materials, such as cadmium, boron, and carbon that absorb neutrons. Like the tape, as the number of control rods increases, the number of free neutrons available for fission reactions decreases.

Solutions to Exercises

1. *Think!*

   • In a fission reaction, a neutron strikes a large nucleus, causing it to split into two smaller nuclei that are usually about the same size. Two or more neutrons are released as well as a large amount of energy.

   Diagram B represents a fission reaction.

2. *Think!*

   • Control rods are made of material that absorbs neutrons.

   • Lowering control rods into a nuclear reactor slows the rate of fission by reducing the number of neutrons available to strike the uranium nuclei.

   Diagram A represents the use of control rods to slow nuclear fission in a nuclear reactor.

11

New Stuff

Chemical Engineering

What You Need to Know

Chemical engineering is the branch of engineering concerned with the chemical properties of substances and how they can be used to make products and packaging for products. **Chemicals** are substances made of one or more elements. You and everything around you such as plants, animals, and this book are made of chemicals. A chemical or a mixture of two or more chemicals that change to form one or more new chemicals undergo a **chemical reaction**. The nuclei of atoms do not change during a chemical reaction. **Chemical properties** are characteristics of a chemical that determines how it chemically reacts.

The starting substance in a chemical reaction is called a **reactant** and the new substance produced is called a **product**. A simple equation to represent a chemical reaction is: reactant → product. The right and left sides of the equation are connected by an arrow (→), a symbol that may be read "yields." The circles in the figure represent two elements that chemically react to form one chemical product. The extended line between the two circles in the products represents a chemical **bond**, which is an attractive force between atoms. **Chemical energy** is the energy needed to form a bond or the energy released when a chemical bond is broken. In a chemical equation, *E* represents energy.

Chemical Reaction

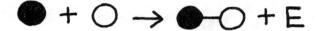

Chemical reactions can be used to make many different kinds of useful products as well as some that are just fun. One example is Silly Putty. Scientists often discover new products while searching for other products. For example, in 1943, James Wright, a scientist for General Electric, was looking for an inexpensive substitute for rubber. Instead, Wright accidentally made a material that would stretch and bounce but was not useful as a rubber substitute or anything else. He wound up selling the rights to a toy store owner, Peter Hodgson, who called the toy Silly Putty and sold it packaged in plastic eggs. In time, the mass production of Silly Putty required the skills of trained chemical engineers.

Sometimes when chemicals are mixed, they do not chemically react. Instead they form a **mixture**, which is a combination of two or more substances that keep their own identity. The different parts in some mixtures do not physically change, such as when different kinds of hard candy are mixed together. In other mixtures, some or all of the parts physically change but still retain their identity. For example, a **solution** is a mixture of a **solute** (what dissolves) with a **solvent** (what the solute dissolves in). In a sugar water solution, sugar is the solute and water is the solvent. Even though not visible, the sugar molecules do not lose their identity. Before sugar and water are combined, the sugar is a white, crystalline solid and the water is a clear liquid. After combining, the mixture is a clear liquid and the sugar crystals appear to have disappeared. This is because the white, solid sugar crystals are broken into sugar molecules, which are too small to see. These invisible molecules are spread throughout the water.

Exercises

1. What type of change is represented by diagram A?

2. What type of change is represented by diagram B?

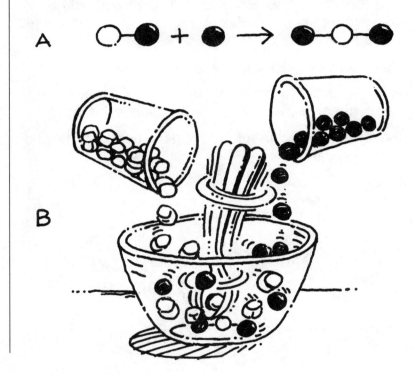

Activity: GOO

Purpose   To use a chemical reaction to make a type of goo.

Materials   4-ounce (120-mL) bottle of Elmer's School Glue—
No Run Gel
1-quart (1-liter) jar
tap water
measuring cup
1-quart (1-liter) bowl
1 teaspoon (5 mL) borax
spoon

Procedure

1. Pour the gel-glue into the jar.

2. Fill the empty glue bottle with water, then pour the water into the jar of glue. Repeat by pouring a second bottle of water into the jar. Stir thoroughly. You have made a glue solution.

3. Pour 1 cup of water into the bowl.

4. Add the borax to the bowl and thoroughly stir until the borax dissolves. You have made a borax solution.

5. Slowly pour the glue solution into the borax solution, stirring as you pour.

Results A thick see-through, semi-solid is produced.

Why? Liquid glue has millions of long chains of molecules called polyvinyl acetate dissolved in water. These molecules act much like cooked spaghetti in that they can easily slip and side over one another in the water. If one molecule is pulled, it can easily separate from the others. This makes the liquid mixture pour easily. Adding the solutions of glue and borax together causes a chemical reaction, resulting in links between the polyvinyl acetate molecules, much like rungs on a ladder connect the sides of the ladder. The individual glue molecules can no longer be separated. Water gets trapped between the links formed by the borax. The resulting soft, rubbery goo breaks if pulled quickly, stretches if pulled slowly, and slowly oozes if placed in your hand and allowed to freely move. If it dries, the trapped water evaporates. Only the linked molecules are left, and the goo is no longer slimy.

The chemical reaction in this experiment produces a goo that has some similarities to the real Silly Putty—both are creepy, slimy, and fun. But different chemicals are combined to make goo and Silly Putty. One big difference between the two products is that unlike goo, Silly Putty doesn't have trapped water, so it doesn't dry out.

Solutions to Exercises

1. *Think!*

- Two separate substances are added, forming one substance. This indicates that something new is formed.

- In a chemical reaction, the reactant(s) changes, producing one or more new chemicals for the product(s).

The change in diagram A represents a chemical reaction.

2. *Think!*

- Two substances are being poured into the bowl and stirred together.

- The substances in the bowl look the same as they look in the glasses.

- A mixture is the combination of two or more substances that keep their separate identities.

- A mixture is an example of a physical change.

A physical change is represented by diagram B.

12

Hot Stuff

Fire Protection Engineering

What You Need to Know

Fire protection engineering is the branch of engineering concerned with designing systems and equipment that prevent or combat fire, such as sprinkler systems in buildings as well as firefighting equipment used by firefighters. Fire protection engineers are also involved in the space program. For example, they design fire safety procedures and equipment for spacecraft.

The three things necessary for a fire to occur are (1) **fuel** (a substance that will burn); (2) **oxygen** (a gas found in air that doesn't burn itself but is needed for other substances to burn); (3) **kindling temperature** (minimum temperature at which a substance will burn). When a match is rubbed on a striking surface, heat due to friction is enough to **ignite** (set on fire) the chemicals on the match head. These chemicals burn only if there is oxygen with which to combine. **Burning** is an **oxidation reaction**, which is a chemical reaction between a substance and oxygen. Oxidation always produces heat energy; the faster the reaction, the more heat produced. Burning is also called **combustion**.

The heat of a fire depends on the speed with which chemicals in a material combine with oxygen. The speed is increased as the oxygen supply increases. For things that are burned in air, which contains about 20 percent oxygen, more oxygen can be made available by reducing the size of the fuel. For example, the pages in a thick book would be more difficult to burn all together than if the pages were torn out and burned separately. This is because the single pages have more surface area for oxygen to surround than when the pages are pressed together in the book. The greater the surface area of a fuel, the easier and faster it will burn. This is why it is easier to burn a large log if it is chopped into small pieces.

A flame is burning gas. For example, when a candle burns, at first the wick burns, causing the solid wax to increase in temperatures and **melt** (change into a liquid). This liquid moves up the wick, and the heat causes the liquid wax to **vaporize** (change into a gas). This gas burns, producing a flame. When a candle is blown out, a trail of smoke can be seen above the wick. Smoke is made of gas and tiny particles from the material being burned. The color of the flame indicates the type of particles in the smoke, which gives firefighters clues about the fuel that is burning.

When the chemicals on a match head ignite, they produce enough energy to heat the wood or paper of the match to its kindling temperature. Slow blowing on a fire adds oxygen and encourages burning. Blowing hard can cool the burning fuel, such as the match, which stops burning if it is cooled. The kindling temperature is not the same for all materials. A fire can be stopped by cooling it, removing the fuel, and/or removing oxygen. A safe campfire is one in which the area around it is cleared of all materials that will burn. When the wood in the campfire burns up, the fire goes out. Even so, no campfire should be left unattended. An unsafe or unattended campfire in a forest could ignite the material around it, causing the unattended fire to continue to spread until there is no more fuel. Fire protection engineers design the processes and materials used to control and stop forest fires—for example, releasing materials from an airplane above the fire to cover the burning fuel and cut off its oxygen supply.

Exercises

1. Which candle, the one in diagram A or the one in diagram B, will burn a longer time?

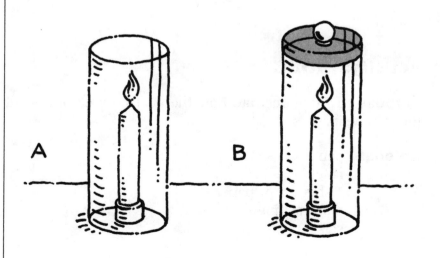

2. Study the figure and select which of the following will cause the action shown to put out the flame:

   a. reducing fuel

   b. reducing temperature below the fuel's kindling temperature

   c. reducing oxygen

Activity: MORE

Purpose To demonstrate how the surface area of a solid fuel can be increased.

Materials pen
ruler
1 sheet copy paper
dishwashing sponge
scissors

Procedure

1. Use the pen and ruler to draw a Surface Data table on the paper, like the one shown below.

Surface Data

Number of Pieces	Number of New Surfaces
1	
2	
3	
4	
5	

2. Count the number of exposed surfaces on the sponge. Record this number in the data table. Note that 0 is recorded for new surfaces.

3. Use the scissors to cut the sponge in half by cutting across the center of the long edge as shown.

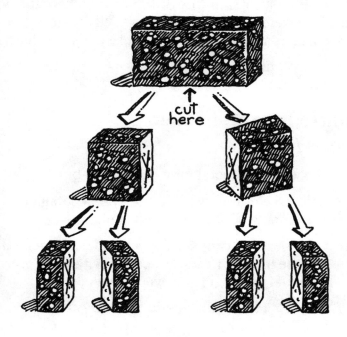

4. Use the marker to make an X on the cut surfaces as shown. The cut surfaces are new, exposed surfaces.

5. Count the newly cut surfaces and record the total number in the data table.

6. Cut each of the two sponge pieces in half as before.

7. Repeat steps 4 and 5.

Results A total of 6 new surfaces are exposed.

Why? When the sponge is cut in half, two new surfaces are exposed. Each time a substance is cut, two new surfaces are exposed. Thus, the surface area of a solid fuel such as coal increases each time it is cut. The greater the surface area, the easier it is for the fuel to combine with oxygen, which makes it easier to burn. Blasting coal out of the ground cuts the solid coal into many pieces and even produces coal dust, which can easily catch on fire. One way that fire protection engineers prevent coal dust fires is to wet the coal with water before blasting. The water causes the dust to stick together, decreasing the surface area. In addition, wet solids are harder to burn.

Solutions to Exercises

1. *Think!*

   • Oxygen is needed for a material to burn.

   • Air is able to move into the open container so that the supply of oxygen is constant.

   • The burning candle in the closed container will use up the oxygen inside the container and go out when the fuel no longer receives oxygen.

   The candle in diagram A will burn longer.

2. *Think!*

- Blowing hard toward the flame cools the wick.

- Kindling temperature is the temperature needed for a substance to burn.

Letter B, reducing temperature below the fuel's kindling temperature, causes the flame to go out.

13

Brighter

Product Development Engineering

What You Need to Know

Product development engineering is the branch of engineering concerned with designing, developing, and testing new products. Some interesting products used by product development engineers are chemicals that cause colors to appear brighter. Chemical brighteners are called **fluorescent brightening agents** or **optical brightening agents**. Optical brighteners capture ultraviolet radiation and change it into visible light, which is emitted. This process is called **fluorescence**.

Product development engineers may use optical brighteners in detergents to make clothes look whiter. While clothes washed with detergent containing optical brightening agents may look whiter, they are not necessarily cleaner. Optical brighteners neither clean nor change the color of cloth. Instead, the tiny particles in the whitener stick to the surface of the cloth. For whitening, optical brighteners are selected that emit visible light in the blue end of the visible spectrum. This bluish light added to the light reflected from the surface of the material produces a bright white appearance. Although these optical brighteners may make your clothes appear brighter, they are chemical **residues** (the solid part left behind) that are purposely left behind on your clothes and may cause skin irritation or other allergic reactions.

Fluorescent ink contains chemicals that absorb ultraviolet (UV) radiation, a high-energy radiation that human eyes cannot see, and these chemicals give off a less energetic radiation called visible light that human eyes can see. In fluorescent highlighters, the color of the ink is also the color of the visible light given off by the UV-absorbing chemical in the ink.

Exercises

1. The letters on the poster are written with fluorescent ink. Which of the lights, A or B, would make the ink forming the letters fluoresce?

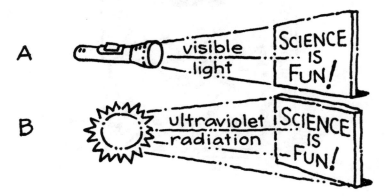

2. Which diagram, A or B, shows that the shirt was washed in detergent containing an optical brightening agent?

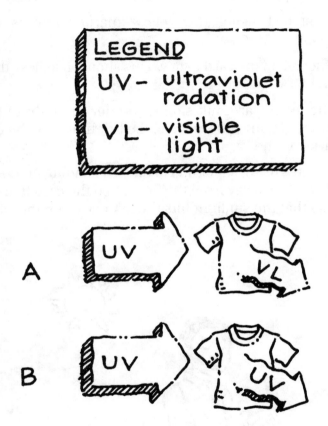

Activity: **EXTRA YELLOW**

Purpose   To determine the effect of sunlight and incandescent light on fluorescent ink.

Materials   fluorescent yellow highlighter marker
white unlined index card
yellow felt-tip marker (not fluorescent)
incandescent lamp

Procedure

1. Use the fluorescent marker to color an area about 1 inch (2.54 cm) square on the index card.

2. Repeat step 1 using the yellow marker that is not fluorescent.

3. Allow the ink on the card to dry. This should take less than 1 minute.

4. Hold the index card, ink side up, under the light of the lamp. Observe any difference in the brightness of the two ink marks on the card.

5. Repeat step 4 using sunlight. Do this by standing outdoors so that you face away from the Sun. Hold the card in front of you so that the sunlight hits the ink marks on the card.

Results Depending on the ink used, the results may vary under the incandescent lamp, but the fluorescent ink is much brighter in sunlight.

Why? The lamp and the Sun both give off visible light, but of the two light sources, the Sun gives off the most ultraviolet radiation. When the different inks are viewed under the lamp, then in sunlight, white light from both light sources strikes the paper. The yellow pigment in both inks reflects the yellow part of the white light. In the sunlight, the particles in the yellow fluorescent ink also absorb ultraviolet radiation and emit yellow light. So there are two sources of yellow light coming to your eye from the fluorescent ink mark: one from yellow pigment and one from the fluorescent particles. This combination causes the ink to appear extra yellow. Under the lamp, one of the inks may look more yellow because it has more yellow pigment, but it is not extra yellow.

Solutions to Exercises

1. *Think!*

   - Fluorescence occurs when ultraviolet light is taken in by a chemical and changed into visible light, which is emitted.

   - Which light gives off ultraviolet rays?

   Light B, showing ultraviolet radiation from the Sun, would cause the ink to fluoresce.

2. *Think!*

   - Optical brightening agents in detergent fluoresce, giving off visible light.

   - Which shirt shows fluorescence, which is the taking in of ultraviolet light and the emitting of visible light?

The shirt in diagram A was washed with a detergent containing an optical brightening agent and therefore shows fluorescence.

14

Primary

Biological Engineering

What You Need to Know

Biology is the study of living things. **Biological engineering** is the branch of engineering concerned with designing methods and products that will create a more healthful living environment for people, animals, and plants.

One job of biological engineers involves food production. They make sure that foods are not only safe to eat but also pleasurable and nutritious by developing ways to control texture and nutrient content during processing.

Proteins are one type of **nutrient** (any substance that living organisms need to grow, produce energy, and stay healthy). The word *protein* is from a Greek word that means "primary." Proteins are very long molecules made of different parts that are connected together. They are often described as being like long chains. **Collagen** makes up almost a third of all the protein in the human body. It is a big, fibrous molecule that connects, strengthens, and supports various parts of the body including skin and bones.

Enzymes are proteins that control chemical reactions in living organisms by causing reactions and changing how fast those reactions occur. Each enzyme has a special shape that allows it to assist in putting specific chemicals together or breaking them apart. It is believed that enzymes act like holders into which molecules of chemicals fit like puzzle pieces.

Some enzymes receive two separate molecules that join and then leave the enzyme together as a single molecule.

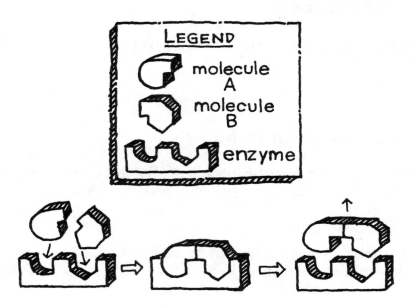

Other enzymes receive a single molecule and bend or twist the molecule, causing it to break apart into separate molecules. These separate molecules then leave the enzyme. The enzymes themselves are not changed by any of these reactions.

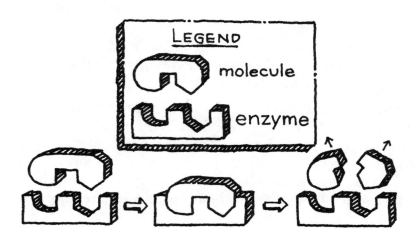

Understanding how enzymes work helps biological engineers to design new processes for building and/or taking apart chemicals to produce useful chemicals. For example, collagen is a long, stiff, fibrous protein that connects and supports many tissues in animals. Collagen is made of three fibers twisted together, much like the fibers in a rope are twisted. The more collagen there is in meat, the tougher the meat. Biological engineers design products containing enzymes that break down the collagen in meat so that the meat will be tender and easier to eat.

Exercise

Observe the figure showing the work of an enzyme. Which part, A, B, C, or D, represents the enzyme?

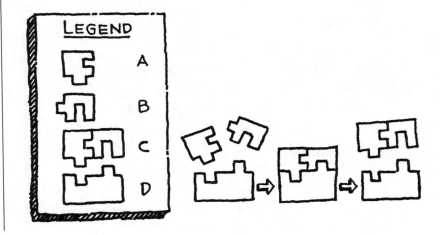

Activity: BREAK UP

Purpose To demonstrate the effect of meat tenderizer on protein.

Materials two 1-ounce (28-g) packets unflavored gelatin
1 teaspoon (5 mL) meat tenderizer
two 3-ounce (90-mL) paper cups
measuring spoon
tap water
red food coloring
2 stirring spoons

Procedure

1. Pour the contents of one of the gelatin packets and the meat tenderizer into one of the cups.

2. Add 2 teaspoons (10 mL) of water and 2 drops of food coloring to the cup.

3. Thoroughly stir the contents of the cup until it is thick. Scoop out the thick mass and place it in your hand. Form the thick mass into a ball. Make note of its firmness and texture, particularly if it is sticky or dry.

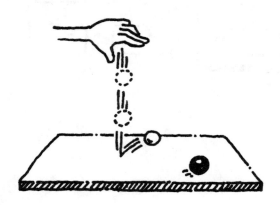

4. Pour the contents of the second gelatin packet into the second cup and add 2 teaspoons (10 mL) of water.

5. Repeat step 3.

6. Allow both balls of gelatin to sit for 3 to 5 minutes. Then lift each and drop them on a table. Make note of how well each ball bounces.

Results The uncolored ball made without meat tenderizer feels dryer and more spongy, and it bounces better than the red ball made with meat tenderizer.

Why? Gelatin is a protein obtained from animal tissues. A common enzyme in meat tenderizer is **papain** (an enzyme extracted from papaya, a tropical fruit). This enzyme breaks apart the gelatin protein. This is why the gelatin mixed with meat tenderizer is not firm.

Solution to Exercise

Think!

- Some enzymes receive separate molecules and help to put the molecules together to form a single molecule.

- Enzymes are not changed by a reaction, meaning they are the same before and after the reaction.

Part D represents the enzyme.

15
Shiny
Metallurgical Engineering

What You Need to Know

Metallurgical engineering is the branch of engineering concerned with metals, which are elements that are usually shiny solids such as silver, gold, and copper. Metals can be formed into sheets or wires and are good conductors of heat and electricity. **Metallurgy** is the science of metals, including understanding their physical and chemical properties, how to remove them from rocks and minerals, and their uses.

A metallurgical engineer generally works in one of these three main branches of metallurgy: chemical, physical, or processes. A **chemical metallurgist** is concerned with the chemical properties of metals and the chemical processes that relate to metals. Chemical processes could include the removal of metals from rocks and minerals, **refining** (the removal of any impurities combined with a metal), and making **alloys** (mixtures of two or more metals or mixtures of one or more metals and a nonmetal, particularly carbon) such as **bronze** (an alloy made of two metals: tin and copper).

A **physical metallurgist** studies the physical properties of metals and their alloys to determine the best methods of processing them into useful products. Physical properties of metals include color, density, hardness, malleability, ductility, and conductivity. **Malleability** is the ability of a substance to be deformed, especially by hammering, or the ability of a substance to be rolled into a thin sheet. **Ductility** is the ability of a substance to be drawn into a wire. **Conductivity** is the ability of a substance to allow either electricity or heat to easily pass through it.

A **process metallurgist** develops and improves the processes that shape metals, such as casting, rolling, drawing, and forging. **Casting** is the shaping of metals by pouring **molten** (liquid) metal into a mold. These products are not usually as strong as those made by forging. **Rolling** shapes a metal into a smooth, flat sheet by moving it between rollers. **Forging** is the hammering or pressing of a metal in order to shape it. Forging makes the metal stronger in the direction that it has been stretched. A blacksmith forges metal into the shape of horseshoes. Metal is shaped into a wire by **drawing**, which means that a large piece of metal is pulled through a small hole. The formed wire has the same diameter as the hole the metal was pulled through.

Chasing pushes a pattern into the surface of a malleable metal. A malleable metal can also be **etched**, which is a

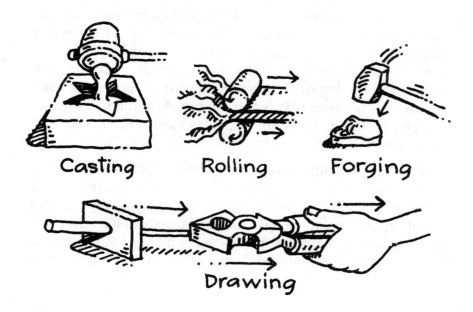

Casting   Rolling   Forging

Drawing

process of forming a pattern on the metal's surface by cutting away part of the surface. In both processes a punch is placed against a metal surface, and the opposite end of the punch is hit with a hammer. For chasing, the punch has a blunt end; for etching, the end is pointed. A modern example of metallurgical engineering is using **ultrasound** (sound vibrations above the normal range of human hearing) to chase or etch a metal surface. Instead of hitting a punch with a hammer, the punch forms the tip of an ultrasonic tool. The punch tip constantly vibrates. When held against a metal surface, the tip deforms the surface.

Exercises

Study the figure of metalworkers to answer the following questions:

1. Tin and copper are examples of metals. Which of these processes is represented by the figure?

   a. casting

   b. drawing

   c. forging

   d. rolling

2. What is the name of the mixture being formed?

Activity: PUNCH DESIGNS

Purpose To determine a method for chasing a malleable metal.

Materials transparent tape
pen
three 4-inch-by-4-inch (10-cm-by-10-cm) squares of aluminum foil
unsharpened pencil
large spoon
6-inch-by-6-inch (15-cm-by-15-cm) square of corrugated cardboard
small towel

Procedure

1. Use the tape and pen to label the three aluminum foil squares: Hard, Medium, and Soft.

2. Lay the foil square labeled Hard on a hard surface such as a table.

3. Hold the pencil upright on the foil with the eraser end up.

4. With the bottom end of the spoon, tap the eraser end of the pencil so that the unsharpened end is pressed into the foil.

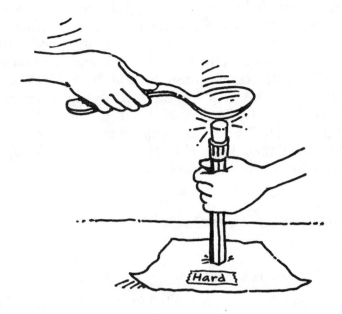

5. Move the pencil to another spot on the foil, then repeat step 4.

6. Lay the foil square labeled Medium on the corrugated cardboard.

7. Repeat steps 3 through 5.

8. Fold the towel in half twice.

9. Lay the foil square labeled Soft on the folded towel.

10. Repeat steps 3 through 5.

11. Compare the depth of the marks made by the pencil on each of the aluminum foil squares.

Results The softer the support for the aluminum foil squares, the deeper the marks made by the pencil. When the towel is used, the foil wrinkles.

Why? Aluminum foil is a malleable metal, which means it can easily be deformed especially when hit or pressed. Chasing is a process of placing a design on a malleable metal. In this experiment, the blunt end of a pencil is hammered into the surface of the sheets of aluminum foil. The depth of the imprint made by the pencil is affected by the firmness of the surface beneath the foil. The softer the surface, the deeper the imprint. To keep the imprint from being too shallow or too deep, metallurgical engineers have to design the best supporting surface for the metal.

Solutions to Exercises

1. *Think!*

   • The metals are molten.

   • The molten metals are being poured into a mold.

   Letter A, casting, is the process being represented.

2. *Think!*

   • Two metals are being mixed together.

   • A mixture of two metals is called an alloy.

   • What is the name of the alloy made by mixing tin and copper?

   Bronze.

16

The Limit

Stress Engineering

What You Need to Know

Stress engineering is the branch of engineering concerned with designing materials that can withstand stress as well as methods for testing stress limits. **Stress** is the force on an area of an object that tends to **deform** it (change its shape). It is also a measure of the force needed to cause deformation of a material. If the force is small, the material undergoes an **elastic deformation**; that is, the material is deformed only while under stress. While the force is being applied, the material is misshapen, but the material returns to its original shape as soon as the force is removed. **Elasticity** is the ability of a material to return to its original size and shape after being deformed.

All materials have an **elastic limit**, which is the maximum force that causes elastic deformation. Forces greater than the elastic limit cause permanent deformation. For example, if you slightly squeeze a plastic cup, then stop squeezing, the cup first changes shape, then returns to its original shape. But if the stress is greater than the elastic limit, the deformation is permanent. In the figure this is expressed as: stress > elastic limit → permanent deformation. **Tensile strength** is the maximum amount of stretching force that a material can withstand without breaking. Tensile strength is the measure of the force on an area of material that pulls the material apart or the stretching force that causes it to break.

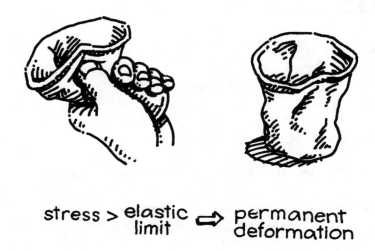

stress > elastic
          limit ⇌ permanent
                  deformation

Materials moving through different machines must be strong enough not to be pulled apart or permanently deformed by stress. For example, a copy machine applies stress on the paper that moves through it. It is important that the paper be strong enough to withstand this force. Stress engineers design ways to test the strength of paper, such as its tensile strength.

Exercise

Study the two diagrams: Before Stress and After Stress. Make note of the rubber band's length in each diagram. Then choose the After Stress diagram, A, B, or C, that indicates the stress was less than the elastic limit of the rubber band.

Before Stress

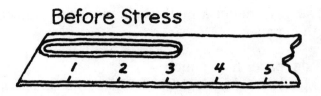

During Stress

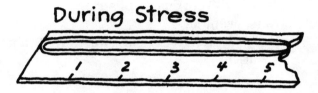

After Stress

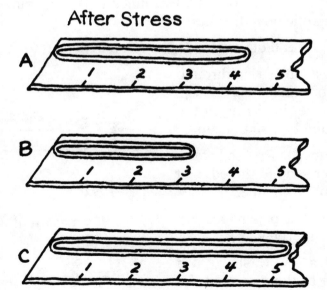

Activity: HOW MUCH?

Purpose To model a method for determining the tensile strength of paper.

Materials paper hole punch
½-by-11-inch (1.25-by-27.5-cm) strip of copy paper
pencil
10-ounce (300-ml) paper cup
12-inch (30-cm) piece of string
transparent tape
thirty ⅜-inch (0.94-cm) washers (quarters will work)

Procedure

1. Use the paper hole punch to cut a hole about ¼ inch (0.63 cm) from one end of the paper strip.

2. Use the pencil to make two holes under the rim of the cup—one on either side.

3. Tie one end of the string through one hole in the cup.

4. Thread the string through the hole in the paper strip, then tie the string in the second hole of the cup.

5. Secure the free end of the paper strip to the edge of a table with tape.

6. Allow the paper and cup to hang freely.

7. Add a few washers at a time to the cup until the string cuts through the paper.

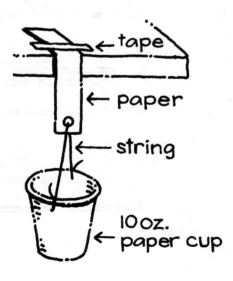

Results The number of washers needed to break the copy paper will vary, but for the author's experiment it took 25.

Why? The weight of the string, cup, and washers pull down on the paper. The paper tears when the stress of this force on the small area inside the hole reaches tensile strength. For the author, the stress force was equal to the weight of the string, cup, and 25 washers. This method of testing the tensile strength of paper can be used to compare the tensile strength of different kinds of paper such as different weights of copy paper and newsprint.

Solution to Exercise

Think!

- The original length of the rubber band before the stress was applied reached the ruler's third mark.

- During stress, the length of the rubber band was greater than the ruler's fifth mark.

- The elastic limit is the maximum force on a material that results in the material returning to its original shape after the force is removed.

- Any stress less than the elastic limit will result in the material returning to its original shape and length, which reaches the ruler's third mark.

Diagram B indicates the stress was less than the elastic limit of the rubber band.

17

Weakened

Product Durability Engineering

What You Need to Know

Product durability engineering is the branch of engineering concerned with designs and processes responsible for product **durability** (a measure of how a product keeps its original qualities and usefulness). People who work with plastics and/or metals are interested in finding new ways to increase the durability of these materials.

Fatigue is commonly used to mean weakness because of repeated motion. If you continually lift a weight, your arms and other muscles in your body will get tired and weaken. But after a rest, you will be ready to lift the weight just as well as before. Unlike your body muscles, fatigue in materials such as metals, plastic, rock, and asphalt is permanent. **Material fatigue** is the weakening of a material often to the point of breaking because of repeated motion. The **fatigue life** of a material is the number of deforming motions that it can endure before breaking. Fatigue life depends on the type of material, the amount of stress on it, and the number of deforming motions. Three types of deforming motions that commonly cause material fatigue are (1) **compressing** (pushing together) and **expanding** (separating of particles, resulting in a larger size), (2) **twisting** (winding), and (3) **flexing** (bending back and forth). A material's resistance to breaking due to material fatigue is called **fatigue resistance**. The greater the fatigue resistance, the greater the fatigue life of a material.

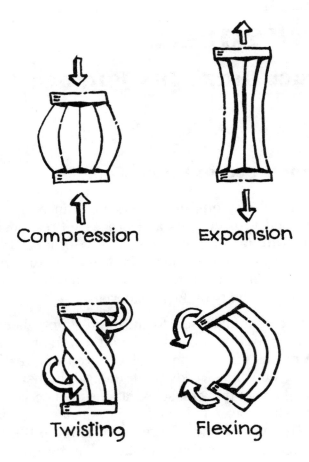

Compression   Expansion

Twisting   Flexing

Accidents have happened because metals fatigue and break. For example, product durability engineers discovered in 1954 that several British airplanes had broken apart and crashed due to the right-angle shape of the metal around the windows. Bending the metal into a right angle caused a small—maybe even microscopic—crack in the metal. Normal flight vibrations, even though small, caused metal fatigue over time in the already weakened metal, which led to breaking. All aircraft windows were immediately redesigned with rounded corners.

Exercises

Wire rope is made of strands of wire. When comparing two wire ropes with equal diameter, the rope with more strands has a greater fatigue resistance. Study the figures to answer the following questions:

1. Which type of wire rope, A or B, has the greatest fatigue life?

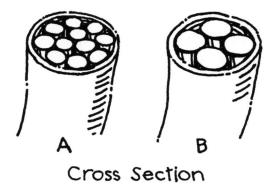

Cross Section

2. Which type of wire rope, C or D, should have the least fatigue life?

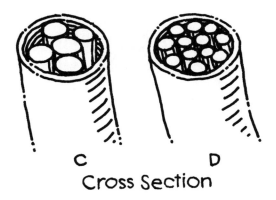

Cross Section

Activity: TIRED

Purpose To demonstrate a method of testing metal fatigue due to bending in a paper clip.

Materials paper clip
transparent tape

Procedure

1. Raise the center small loop of the paper clip so that it is perpendicular (at a 90° angle) to the larger loop.

2. Tightly secure the larger loop to a table with several layers of tape.

3. Return the small loop to its original position by pushing it down so that it touches the larger loop.

4. Raise the loop so that it is perpendicular to the table, then lower it to its original position. Continue until the metal breaks. Count each up-and-down motion as one cycle. *Caution: Do not touch the part of the paper clip that is being bent, because it gets hot.*

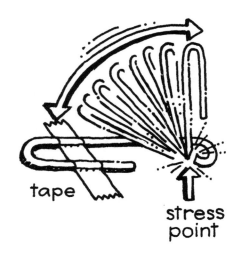

tape

stress
point

Results The paper clip breaks at the point where it moves back and forth. The number of cycles needed to break the clip varies, depending on the type and size of the paper clip. The author's paper clip took 12½ flexes to break when opened 90°.

Why? Bending the metal first weakens it, then continued motion causes it to break. The fatigue process starts with a crack in the metal so small that it can be seen only with a microscope. With repeated bending, the crack widens. The damage is **cumulative**, meaning it adds up. Each bend causes damage, and resting doesn't return the metal to its original undamaged condition. The number of bends resulting in breakage varies depending on various factors such as the type of material and the amount of stress applied.

Solutions to Exercises

1. *Think!*

   - A wire rope is made of strands of wire. The more strands, the greater is the rope's fatigue resistance.

   - The greater the fatigue resistance, the greater is the material's fatigue life.

   - The ropes are of equal diameter, but A has more strands of wire.

   Wire rope type A has the greatest fatigue life.

2. *Think!*

   - Wire rope D has the greatest number of strands of wire and the greatest fatigue resistance.

   - Wire rope C has the least number of strands of wire and the least fatigue resistance.

   - The less the fatigue resistance, the less the fatigue life.

   - The rope with the least number of strands of wire has the least fatigue resistance.

   Wire rope C has the least fatigue life.

18

Discarded

Environmental Engineering

What You Need to Know

Environmental engineering is the branch of engineering concerned with designing things and processes to improve the environment. The **environment** is the surroundings of an organism; that is, living and nonliving things that affect the life, development, and survival of an organism. Environmental engineers deal with the prevention and treatment of air and water **pollution** (anything that destroys the purity of a substance, making it not useful) and **waste disposal** (the process of getting rid of **waste**—unwanted things).

Solid waste includes **garbage** (indoor waste) such as from businesses, schools, and homes, as well as **yard waste** (waste from outdoors) such as leaves, grass cuttings, and twigs. In the United States, paper is the number one solid waste material, making up about 40 percent of discarded trash. Thus, for every 100 pounds of trash thrown away, about 40 pounds is paper. There are many different kinds of paper, from glossy magazine pages, newspapers, and junk mail to stuffing in diapers, paper cups, and cardboard packaging. The rest of the solid waste in decreasing order of percentage discarded is yard waste, food waste, glass, metal, plastic, and other materials including cloth and rubber.

About 75 percent of waste is buried in **landfills** (areas where waste is buried), and the remainder is **incinerated** (burned until it turns to ash) or **recycled** (made into new products). An **open landfill** is a hole in which waste is dumped. Open landfills are dirty and smelly, attracting insects, rats, and other animals. They are now being closed because of their unsanitary conditions.

Environmental engineers have designed **sanitary landfills**, which are cleaner areas for disposing of solid waste. Like an open landfill, a sanitary landfill is a hole in the ground, but the hole is very deep. Unlike an open landfill, a sanitary landfill has a specially designed liner or multiple liners made of clay, thick plastic, or a combination of materials. The liner protects the environment from **leachate** (a liquid that percolates through a material). Leachate in landfills is formed by rainwater that **percolates** (moves through the spaces in a material) through the soil and the waste in the landfill, mixing with some of the materials in the waste. This liquid waste can be harmful to humans and animals. Without the liner in the landfill, the liquid waste could enter **groundwater** (underground water) that supplies drinking water to wells and springs. With the liner, the harmful leachate is trapped in the bottom of the landfill until it is pumped out and treated so that it can be safely added to lakes and streams.

Some materials in landfills are **biodegradable**; that is, they are capable of being decomposed by microorganisms. **Decomposition** is a type of chemical reaction in which chemicals break apart, forming smaller chemicals. The gases formed by decomposition can build up and eventually escape into the air above the landfill. To prevent these gases from polluting the air, the gases are collected and some are used as fuel.

Each day, trash in landfills is spread out, **compacted** (pressed together), and covered with soil. The dirt layer provides a barrier to help guard against critters and odors. When a landfill is full, a clay cap is put over it. Soil is then placed over the cap, and grass, plants, and trees are planted on top. The leachate and gas produced in the covered trash is monitored for years after the landfill is closed. Closed landfills can be turned into parks or other recreation areas.

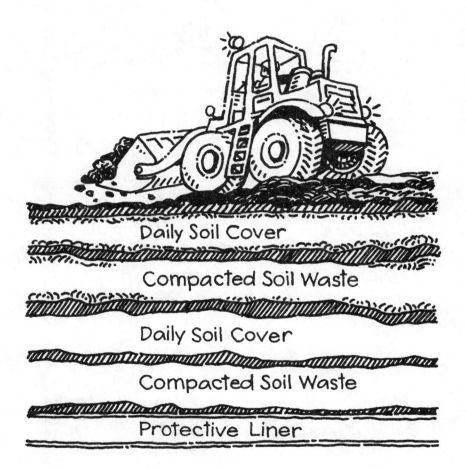

Daily Soil Cover

Compacted Soil Waste

Daily Soil Cover

Compacted Soil Waste

Protective Liner

Exercises

1. Identify the three common methods of waste disposal shown in figures A, B, and C.

A   Trash   Incinerator

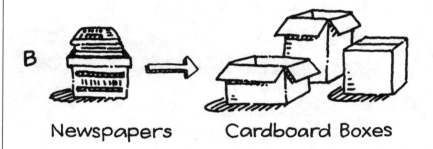

B   Newspapers   Cardboard Boxes

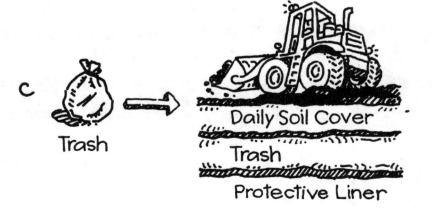

C   Trash   Daily Soil Cover

Trash

Protective Liner

2. Which figure, A or B, represents a possible use of a closed landfill?

A

B

Activity: TILTED

Purpose To model how leachate is collected in a landfill.

Materials 12-by-12-inch (30-by-30-cm) piece of aluminum foil
sheet of copy paper
10-ounce (300-mL) transparent plastic cup
blue food coloring
4 tablespoons (60 mL) dirt
¼ cup (63 ml) tap water

Procedure

1. Tear the aluminum foil and sheet of paper into 8 to 12 small pieces. Wad each piece into a ball.

2. Place half of the aluminum balls into the cup. Then add half of the paper balls. Repeat with the remaining aluminum and paper balls, making four layers in all.

3. With your fingers, press down on the aluminum and paper balls, squeezing them as tightly together as possible without breaking the cup.

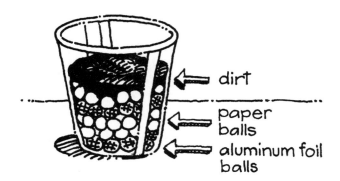

4. Add 4 to 6 drops of food coloring to the cup.

5. Add the dirt to the cup, spreading it evenly over the contents.

6. Pour the water into the cup.

7. Observe the movement of the water through each layer.

8. After 2 to 3 minutes, tilt the cup and observe where the drained water at the bottom collects.

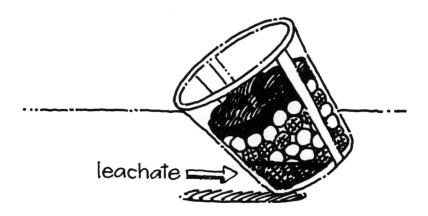

leachate

Results The water mixes with the blue food coloring, and the mixture drains to the bottom of the cup. When the cup is tilted, the water mixture collects at the lowest end.

Why? The cup represents the liner of a landfill. The aluminum and paper balls in the cup represent the daily collection of trash with a layer of dirt over it. Pressing down on the simulated trash represents the crushing of trash in a landfill so that the trash takes up the least amount of space. The water represents rain that falls on the surface and percolates through the different layers. The blue food coloring represents substances in the soil and the waste that mix with the rainwater. This mixture collects on the bottom of the landfill (the bottom of the glass). Tilting the glass makes most of the leachate collect in one area. One way that engineers design landfills is to tilt them at the bottom so that the leachate collects in the lowest part and can be pumped out through pipes.

Solutions to Exercises

1. *Think!*

- Figure A shows trash being burned. What is the name of the process by which waste is burned?

- Figure B shows trash in the form of newspapers being changed into cardboard boxes. What is the name of the process in which a new product is made from an old one?

- Figure C shows trash being buried. What is the name of the area where trash is buried?

The three methods of waste disposal are incineration (figure A), recycling (figure B), and a sanitary landfill (figure C).

2. *Think!*

- Figure A is a pond. Digging in a landfill to create a hole for a pond would uncover the buried trash.

- Figure B is a park. Trees and other plants can be grown on the covered surface of a closed landfill.

Figure B represents a possible use of a closed landfill.

19

Less Is More

Geotechnical Engineering

What You Need to Know

Geotechnical engineering is the branch of engineering concerned with properties of the ground. Geotechnical engineers look for ways to prevent erosion in regions where structures, such as buildings, roadways, tunnels, and bridges will be built. **Erosion** is the breakdown and removal of a material's particles by natural processes such as water and wind. Construction of roads, bridges, tunnels, buildings, or any development that causes the soil to be cut open, laid bare, or compacted causes erosion. Exposed soil is easily blown away by wind or washed away by rain.

The more compacted (pressed together) the soil, the less **porous** (having spaces between particles) it is. Instead of rain sinking into compacted soil, water tends to run across and wash away the soil. One way that geotechnical engineers deal with soil erosion is to build barriers such as by placing hay bales on inclines to slow and trap water and soil. Another method of stopping or slowing soil erosion is to cover the bare soil with a mixture of grass seeds and fertilizer, then cover the seed mixture with straw, hay, wood chips, bark, or any material that will prevent the seeds and soil from being blown or washed away. In some circumstances, soil erosion is decreased by increasing soil porosity, such as by mixing soils made of different-size particles.

Soil porosity is due to **soil texture**, which is the physical property of soil describing the size of its particles. The three types of soil particles in increasing order of size are clay, silt, and sand. **Clay** particles are less than 0.002 mm in diameter, **silt** particles are between .002 and .05 mm in diameter, and **sand** starts with 0.05 mm for fine sand to 2.0 mm in diameter for very coarse sand. Fine-textured soils have a large amount of clay, which are the smaller soil particles. Course-textured soil is more sandy because of the larger particles.

The contacts made between soil particles create **pores** (spaces between the particles of a material). Large sand particles create large pores while small clay particles create small pores. But a soil sample with small particles and small pores might have as much total pore space as an equal-volume sample of large particles with large pores. This is because the smaller particles create more pores. It is the amount of pore space and not the particle size that causes **porosity** (a measure of how porous a material is). Particles come in many shapes and sizes. The porosity of any soil depends on how its particles pack together. As shown, particles of the same size can create different pore sizes depending on how the particles are stacked together. Also, mixtures of different sizes of particles decrease porosity because they pack together, reducing the number and/or size of pores.

High Porosity

Medium Porosity

Low Porosity

Exercises

1. Which figure, A or B, is more porous?

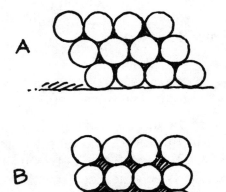

2. Which figure, A, B, or C, represents particles in a low-porosity soil?

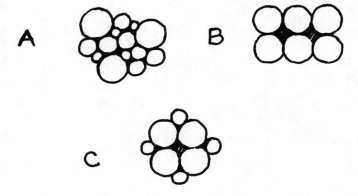

Activity: FILL 'ER UP

Purpose To determine how mixing soil with different-size particles affects the porosity of a mixture.

Materials ½ (125 mL) dry uncooked rice
1-cup (250-mL) measuring cup
25 marbles

Procedure

1. Pour the rice into the measuring cup.

2. Carefully place the marbles on top of the rice in the measuring cup until the top of the marbles are at the 1-cup mark. Compare the space size between the marbles and the space size between the rice grains.

3. Note the measuring level of the marbles in the cup.

4. With your fingers, push the marbles into the rice so that as little as possible of the marbles appear at the surface of the rice. Note any space between the marbles.

5. Note the measuring level of the marble and rice mixture in the cup.

Results Before mixing, the top of the marble layer is at about the 1-cup (250-mL) mark. The space size between the marbles is larger than that between the rice grains. After mixing, the marble and rice mixture is at about the ¾-cup (189-mL) mark. The space that was between the marbles before mixing is now mostly filled with rice.

Why? Before mixing, the total volume of the rice and the marbles is about ½ cup (125 mL) each. There are only 25 marbles but hundreds of rice grains. The marbles are much larger than the rice grains, and when separate, the space between the marbles is much greater than between the rice grains. When mixed together, the smaller grains of rice are able to fill most of the spaces between the marbles. Thus, the mixture has less porosity and takes up less space than when the marbles and rice were separate.

Solutions to Exercises

1. *Think!*

   - The larger the pores, the more porous a material.

   - Which figure has more pores?

   Figure B is more porous.

2. *Think!*

   - Soils that are compacted have low porosity.

   - Mixtures of different-size particles pack together.

   The soil represented in figure A is more compacted, so it would be the least porous.

20
Flowing Through
Hydraulic Engineering

What You Need to Know

Hydraulic engineering is the branch of engineering concerned with the flow and transporting of fluids, primarily water. Some hydraulic engineers design systems for controlling the rate of water flow so that water can be transported for use such as drinking or for converting water power into electricity.

Flow rate is the amount of fluid that passes through an opening in a given amount of time. Flow rate can be calculated using this formula: $FR = V \div t$. FR represents flow rate, V represents **volume** (the amount of space occupied by a substance) of the fluid, and t represents time. For example, if 6 gallons of water flow through a pipe in 2 hours, the flow rate would be: 6 gallons ÷ 2 hours = 3 gallons/hour. The flow rate of 3 gallons/hour is read "3 gallons per hour."

Hydraulic engineers design water systems so that homes and businesses are supplied with water. They must first consider how much water is needed, then determine the necessary flow rate of water to supply the needed amount. They must understand things that affect flow rate such as the size of the pipes the water moves through. More water can flow through a pipe with a large diameter than one with a smaller diameter. Thus, as the diameter of a pipe increases, the flow rate of water or any other liquid passing through it increases.

Friction between a fluid and surfaces through which it flows is also a consideration of a hydraulic engineer. The greater the friction, the slower the fluid moves; thus, the flow rate decreases. For example, water flowing through a pipe has different speeds. The water very near the pipe walls travels more slowly than the water in the very center of the pipe. This is due to friction between the pipe and the water touching it. The same is true of water flowing through open ditches or rivers. Considering only the effect of the friction between the water and the ground, the speed of the water would be faster in the very center where it is not touching the ground under or on the sides of the ditch or stream.

A hydraulic engineer must also consider the pressure on the moving fluid. In water systems, the pressure can be controlled by a mechanical pump. As the pressure on a fluid increases, the flow rate increases.

Exercises

1. In which pipe, A or B, would water have the greatest flow rate?

A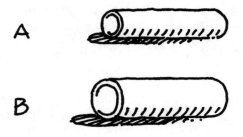

B

2. Determine the flow rate if 40 liters of water passes out of a pipe every 4 hours.

Activity: MORE

Purpose To demonstrate how the diameter of an opening affects the flow rate of water passing through it.

Materials sharpened pencil
5-ounce (150-mL) paper cup
2 sheets of paper towels
2 small bowls of equal size
tap water

Procedure

1. Use the pencil to make a small hole in the side of the cup near the bottom. Do this by inserting only the sharpened lead of the pencil into the cup.

2. Make a second hole, at the same level but larger than the first hole, about halfway around the cup. Do this by inserting the pencil so that the largest part of the pencil is pushed through the cup.

3. Spread the paper towel sheets on a table.

4. Set the bowls, side by side, on the paper towels with the rims touching.

5. With your fingers over the holes in the cup, fill the cup with water.

6. Hold the cup about 2 inches (5 cm) above where the rims of the bowls touch. Each hole in the cup should be pointing at one of the bowls.

7. Holding the top of the cup, remove your fingers from over the holes. Water will pour from the holes into the separate bowls. Move the cup as needed so that the water from each hole flows only into one bowl. Measure the amount of water collected in each bowl.

Results The bowl collecting water flowing out of the smaller hole has less water than the bowl collecting water from the larger hole.

Why? Variables (things that can change) that can affect the flow rate of fluids include friction, pressure, time, the size of the hole the water flows through, and viscosity. **Viscosity** is a measure of the ability of a fluid to flow; the higher the viscosity, the slower the fluid flows. In this activity, the same fluid, water, is flowing out of two different-size holes at the same depth in one cup at the same time. So viscosity, friction, pressure, and time are the same for both streams of water. The only variable affecting the flow rate is hole size. Since less water flows out of the smaller hole than the larger one in the same amount of time, the flow rate is less for the smaller hole. This is true for fluids moving through pipes if the other variables affecting flow rate are the same. Engineers often use laboratory models such as the one in this experiment to study flow rates.

Solutions to Exercises

1. *Think!*

   - Flow rate is a measure of the amount of fluid such as water that passes by a point or through an opening in a certain amount of time.

   - More water can pass through a pipe with a large diameter than one with a smaller diameter. Thus, water flowing through a pipe with a larger diameter will have a greater flow rate.

   Water in pipe B would have the greatest flow rate.

2. *Think!*

   - Flow rate can be calculated using this formula: $FR = V \div t$. FR represents flow rate, V represents volume of the fluid, and t represents time.

   - For the problem, FR = 40 liters ÷ 4 hours.

   The flow rate is 10 liters/hour, which is read 10 liters per hour.

21

Shake Up

Earthquake Engineering

What You Need to Know

Earthquake engineering is the branch of engineering concerned with the effects of earthquakes, including reducing harmful effects of earthquakes on structures such as roads, bridges, and buildings. An **earthquake** is a shaking of the ground caused by a sudden movement of rock beneath Earth's surface. The spot below Earth's surface where vibrations (back-and-forth movement) from an earthquake begin is called the **hypocenter**. The point on Earth's surface

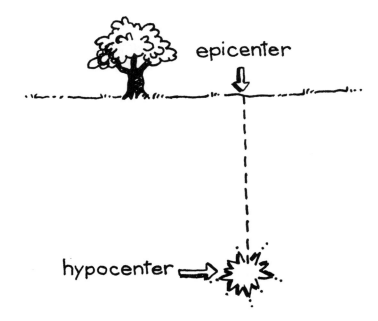

directly above the hypocenter is called the **epicenter**. The epicenter generally receives the strongest and the longest shaking from an earthquake. Two common motions resulting from an earthquake are **lateral vibrations** (side-to-side motion) and **vertical vibrations** (up-and-down motion).

The size of an earthquake can be measured using the Richter scale and the Mercalli scale. The **Richter scale** is a number system used to measure the **magnitude** (the amount of energy released) of an earthquake. The scale is a set of numbers between 1 and 9. The energy increases by a multiple of 32 times from one whole number to the next. For example, an earthquake with a Richter magnitude of 7 releases 32 times as much energy as one with a magnitude of 6. An earthquake with a magnitude of 7 has 1,024 (32×32) times as much energy as an earthquake with a magnitude of 5.

The **Mercalli scale** is a measurement of an earthquake's **intensity**, which is the amount of destruction of structures and the deaths and injuries of people caused by an earthquake. The intensity is usually greatest near the epicenter. But this is not always true, because damage varies according to the nature of the ground and the stability of the structures.

Earthquake engineers use models to determine how different structures will behave during an earthquake. Things to consider are shapes as well as building materials. For example, buildings with a square or a rectangular shape do better than those with other shapes such as L, T, or H shapes. Buildings made of ductile materials such as aluminum or steel, which can be stretched without breaking, perform better than buildings made of **brittle** (easily broken) materials.

Exercises

1. Study the movement of the building during an earthquake and determine if the ground motion is lateral or vertical.

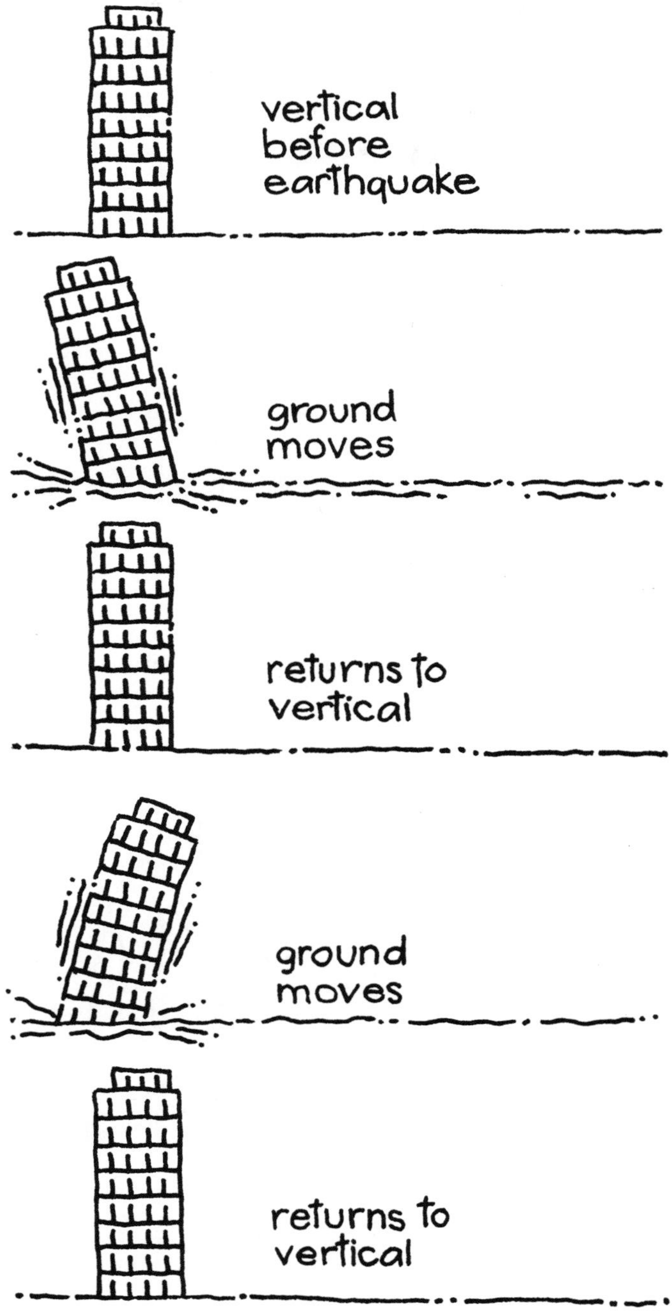

vertical
before
earthquake

ground
moves

returns to
vertical

ground
moves

returns to
vertical

2. How much more energy does an earthquake with a Richter scale reading of 5 have than one with a reading of 2?

Activity: SIDE-TO-SIDE

Purpose   To demonstrate the response of buildings to lateral vibrations produced by earthquakes.

Materials   1 washcloth
               Slinky

Procedure

1. Spread the washcloth on a table about 12 inches (30 cm) from the table's edge.

2. Stand the Slinky on the washcloth.

3. Grab the edge of the washcloth with your fingers and quickly pull the cloth forward about 6 inches (15 cm).

4. Observe the movement of the Slinky.

Results The bottom of the Slinky is pulled to the side. The top section of the Slinky temporarily lags behind, then springs back into place.

Why? The bottom of the coil is pulled to the side by the movement of the cloth beneath it. A similar movement occurs during an earthquake, when the ground below a building has lateral vibrations. Lateral vibrations are very destructive, since they cause the walls to bend to one side, then the other side. Inertia (the tendency of an object at rest to remain at rest) holds the upper part of the coil or a building in a leaning position for a short time, then the structure snaps back into its original position. Next it bends to the opposite side, then snaps back to its original position. During a typical earthquake lasting only 15 seconds, a building may bend and snap between 15 and 100 times, depending on its structure.

Solutions to Exercises

1. *Think!*

   - The ground appears flat in each diagram.

   - When the ground moves, the building leans to one side, then the other. This indicates that the ground is moving sideways.

   The motion of the ground is lateral.

2. *Think!*

   - Between each whole number on the Richter scale, the energy increases by a multiple of 32.

   - There is a difference of 3 whole numbers between the numbers 2 and 5. So the energy increase is $32 \times 32 \times 32$.

   An earthquake with a Richter scale reading of 5 has 32,768 times more energy than one with a reading of 2.

22

Changes

Meteorological Engineering

What You Need to Know

Meteorological engineering is the branch of engineering concerned with designing and testing meteorological equipment used for sensing, detecting, measuring, recording, and displaying weather conditions. **Meteorology** is the study of **weather**, which is the changes in conditions in the lower atmosphere of Earth, including changes in the temperature, humidity, and pressure of air, as well as the direction and speed of wind.

Meteorological equipment includes thermometers, barometers, and anemometers. A **thermometer** is an instrument used for measuring **temperature** (how hot or cold a material is). Two of the thermometer scales used in meteorology are Celsius and Fahrenheit. In the United States, the Fahrenheit scale is more commonly used. On this scale, 32°F (read 32 degrees Fahrenheit) is the temperature at which pure water freezes, and 212°F is the temperature at which it boils. Most air temperature falls within this range but not all.

A **barometer** is an instrument used to measure **air pressure**, which is the force of air on surfaces due to the motion of air molecules. Air pressure is not the same everywhere. Factors that affect air pressure include temperature and **altitude** (height above sea level). As air temperature decreases, air particles move slower and are closer together, so cold air is more **dense** (many particles of a substance in a small space)

boiling point
of water
212°F

freezing
point of
water
32°F

than hot air. A column of cold air is more dense, so it has more particles of air than a hotter air column. Even though colder air particles move slower and hit with less force than hot air particles, more cold particles hit the surface. So the colder the temperature of air, the greater its pressure.

Air particles are most dense at sea level and decrease in density with altitude. This is because the air particles at the bottom of an air column have more air pressing down; thus, the weight of the air above presses the particles closer together, making them more dense. At high altitudes such as on a mountaintop the air is said to be thin, meaning there are fewer air particles than at sea level. The air pressure of this air is less than at sea level.

Changes in air pressure in a specific area are used to help predict the weather. A decrease in air pressure is often a sign of rain, whereas an increase is often a sign of sunny skies.

Wind is the horizontal movement of air in relation to Earth's surface. **Anemometers** are instruments used to measure the speed of wind.

Exercises

1. Which figure, A or B, is more likely to be a region with decreasing air pressure?

A

B

2. According to temperature, which diagram, A or B, is best for a summer day?

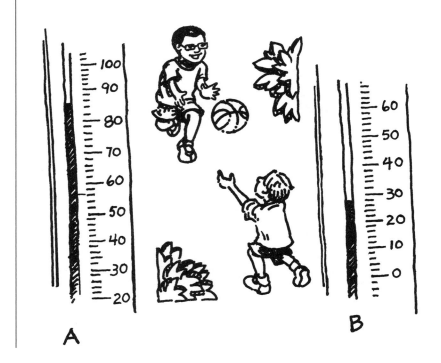

Activity: SPINNER

Purpose To make an anemometer.

Materials drawing compass
6-inch-by-6-inch (15-cm-by-15-cm) piece of poster
  board
scissors
marking pen
transparent tape
12-inch (30-cm) piece of sewing thread
Ping-Pong ball

Procedure

1. Use the compass to draw a curved line connecting two diagonal corners of the piece of poster board as shown in the diagram.

2. Cut along the curved line and keep the cone-shaped piece of poster board. Discard the rest.

3. Prepare a scale on the curved edge of the poster board by marking nine evenly spaced sections along the curved edge. Number them, starting with one as shown in the diagram.

4. Tape the poster board to the top edge of the ruler as shown. If the ruler has print only on one side, tape the poster board to the side without print.

5. Tape one end of the thread to the Ping-Pong ball.

6. Tape the other end of the thread near the corner of the poster board. The thread should hang so that it crosses the zero mark on the poster board.

7. Stand outside in a windy area. Hold the ruler horizontal and point it in the direction from which the wind is blowing.

8. Observe where the string crosses the poster board scale.

Results In a gentle breeze, the string moves slightly from its vertical position. A faster breeze causes the string to move farther up the scale.

Why? Your Ping-Pong ball anemometer can be used to compare but not measure wind speed. The speed of the wind hitting the ball is indicated by the position of the string across the poster board scale. The higher the number, the faster the wind is blowing.

Solutions to Exercises

1. *Think!*

   - Decreasing air pressure is generally associated with rain.

   Figure B is more likely to be a region with decreasing air pressure.

2. *Think!*

   - Summer days are generally the hottest days during the year.

   - The higher the temperature, the hotter the day.

   Diagram A best represents the temperature of a summer day.

23
Around and Around
Hydrology Engineering

What You Need to Know

Hydrology engineering is the branch of engineering concerned with water in Earth's atmosphere as well as water on and beneath Earth's surface. A major concern for hydrologic engineers is Earth's **water cycle**; that is, the processes involved in the movement of water between Earth and its atmosphere. Water cycle processes include precipitation, evaporation, transpiration, condensation, interception, infiltration, and runoff.

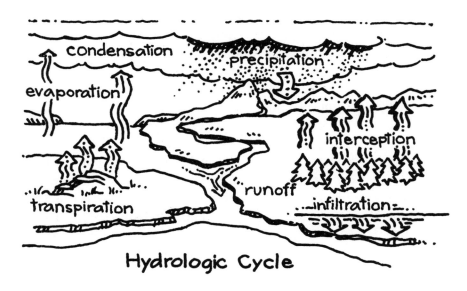

Hydrologic Cycle

Depending on temperature, water in the atmosphere is in a liquid or a **vapor** (gas form of a substance that is usually in liquid form). An increase in temperature, which is an increase in energy, causes liquid water to vaporize (the process of a substance changing into a gas). A decrease in temperature, which is a decrease in energy, can cause water vapor to **condense** (change from a gas to a liquid). Tiny suspended particles such as dust encourage condensation. When particles of water vapor hit cool dust particles, they cling to the dust particles and to each other, forming a tiny, invisible drop of liquid water. Many of these tiny drops of water form **clouds** (visible masses of water drops that float in the atmosphere), which are moved from one place to another by winds. Eventually the water drops in clouds become too large and heavy to float in air, and they fall as **precipitation** (liquid and solid forms of water that fall from the atmosphere). The primary sources of water in the water cycle are the oceans, which contain about 97 percent of Earth's water supply. Also, water gains energy and **evaporates** (changes from a liquid into a gas) from other sources such as lakes, rivers, and moist soil, and water is given off by plants, mostly through leaves, in a process called **transpiration**.

About 75 percent of precipitation falls back into the oceans. But due to **advection** (movement of water in any form through the atmosphere) the remaining 25 percent falls over land. Some of this precipitation collects on the surface of objects, such as plants and buildings, and eventually evaporates without reaching the ground. This process is called **interception**. Several things happen to the precipitation that reaches land. Some of it evaporates. In cold areas, snow and ice can remain on the ground for short or long periods before eventually melting. Rainwater soaks into the ground. **Infiltration** is the process by which water moves from the surface into the ground. This water, called groundwater (all water beneath Earth's surface) is used by plants, and it supplies wells and springs with water. The rate of infiltration is influenced by several things, including the physical characteristics of the soil,

soil cover, and rainfall intensity. Hydrologic engineers design ways to recharge groundwater, which is the addition of water to groundwater by natural or artificial processes.

Liquid water from precipitation that is unable to soak into the ground and that moves over its surface is called **runoff**. This moving water generally causes erosion (process by which materials are broken into smaller parts and moved) of the surface over which it flows. Runoff can carry pollutants it picks up to streams, lakes, and other water supplies. One of the many jobs of hydrologic engineers is to design instruments and/or methods to measure runoff. They are also involved in the design and construction of structures to control runoff.

Exercises

1. Which figure, A or B, represents transpiration?

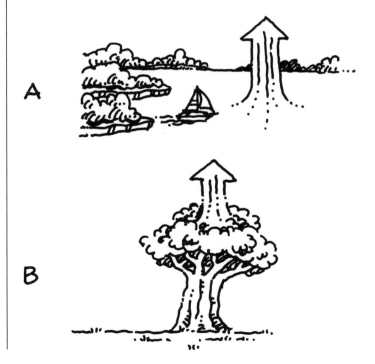

2. Study the following equations and determine which represents the condensation process of water:

a. liquid water + energy → water vapor

b. water vapor – energy → liquid water

c. ice + energy → liquid water

Activity: COVERED

Purpose To determine the effect of ground cover on interception.

Materials scissors
two 5-ounce (150-mL) paper cups
4 facial tissues
½ cup (125 mL) dry leaves
3 to 4 sheets of newspaper
spray bottle
tap water
red food coloring

Procedure

1. Cut the bottom out of both paper cups.

2. Wad one tissue and place it in the bottom of one of the cups. Wad a second tissue and add it to this cup. Push the tissues down so that they fill about half of the cup but do not extend out the bottom opening.

3. Repeat step 2, placing two tissues in the remaining cup.

4. Add the leaves to one of the cups. Hold your hand over the bottom of the cup so that the tissues do not come out as you press the leaves into the cup.

5. Spread the newspaper sheets on a table and set the cups in the center of the newspaper.

6. Fill the spray bottle about half full with water.

7. Add 10 to 15 drops of food coloring to the water in the bottle. Gently shake the bottle to mix the water and the food coloring. Add more coloring if needed to make the H_2O a dark red. Place the spraying lid on the bottle. Squeeze the nozzle several times into a sink or outdoors until the colored water easily sprays out.

8. Spray into each of the cups three times. Make sure the sprayer is the same distance above each cup and that the spray is straight down on the cups.

9. Lift the cup of tissue only and hold it over the newspaper. Pull the tissues out of the bottom hole. Open the tissues and observe the amount of red water on them.

10. Repeat step 9 using the cup of tissue and leaves.

Results The uncovered tissues have more red water staining them than the tissues that were covered with leaves.

Why? The tissues represent the ground. In areas where there is a great amount of ground cover, such as dried leaves as in this experiment as well as grass and other plants, there is more interception of precipitation. This is demonstrated by the amount of staining of the tissues covered with leaves. The red water sprayed onto the leaves represents precipitation. The leaves intercept, which means they block all or most of the passage of the precipitation. Thus, the ground (tissues) receives little to none of the falling colored water.

Solutions to Exercises

1. *Think!*

   • Transpiration is the process by which plants lose water, mostly from their leaves.

   Figure B represents transpiration.

2. *Think!*

   • Condensation is the change from a gas to a liquid.

   • Condensation occurs when a gas loses energy.

   Equation B represents the condensation process of water.

24

Neighbors

Agricultural Engineering

What You Need to Know

Agricultural engineering is the branch of engineering concerned with the production of agricultural products in the quantity and quality needed by today's consumers. **Agriculture** is the raising of plants and animals for food, feed, fiber, fuel, and other useful products.

Agricultural engineers who work with plant production must have an understanding of how plants affect each other. For example, some plants release **allelochemicals**, which are chemicals that inhibit the growth of other plants. Some plants release allelochemicals from their roots. Nearby plants absorb these chemicals from the soil and die.

Knowing which plants are affected by different allelochemicals is important not only in determining which plants can be grown near each other but in developing ways to control weeds. A **weed** is generally thought to be any plant that grows where it is not wanted. A rose growing in a cornfield would be considered a weed. Agricultural engineers are involved in the management of weed control, which includes using organic weed killers. An organic weed killer contains natural materials instead of synthetic chemicals. For example, corn **gluten** (protein in grains) is used to kill some weeds including crabgrass and dandelions. When added to the soil, the corn gluten breaks down, forming allelochemicals that inhibit root development on the germinating seeds of crab-grass and dandelions. Without roots, the plant cannot develop and it dies.

Some agricultural engineers are involved in the transportation of **crops** (the yield from plants in a single growing season). It is important for them to know that some crops, such as fruit, produce and release ethylene gas into the air during their ripening process. Ethylene works like a switch that turns on the production of other chemicals inside the fruit, each speeding a specific part of the ripening process. While cooling the fruit slows the ripening process by these chemicals, it does not stop the production of ethylene gas. Today fruit can be quickly ripened by placing it in a closed room with ethylene gas circulating around. To delay the ripening process, the fruit can be stored in cold temperatures while the air in the room is cycled through charcoal filters to absorb any ethylene made by the fruit. Information about the effects of ethylene gas help engineers to design better ways of packaging and transporting foods that release this gas.

Green Apples   Red Apples

Exercises

1. In which figure, A or B, will the fruit ripen fastest?

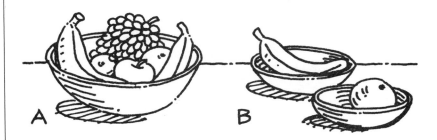

2. Corn and sunflower plants are both grown for food crops. In which of the figures is a sunflower plant a weed?

Activity: BAG IT

Purpose To determine how placement in a sealed bag affects the speed at which a banana ripens.

Materials 3 unripe equal-size bananas (bananas should be the same shade of green or yellow-green)
paper lunch bag

Procedure

1. Place one banana in each of the plastic bags.

2. Fold over the top of one of the bags and leave the other bag open.

3. Set the bags side by side on an indoor table, and lay the third banana next to the bags.

Open Air   Open Paper Bag   Closed Paper Bag

4. Observe and record the color of the bananas each day at about the same time for 3 or more days. Note how much the appearance of each banana changes—for example, "mostly green with yellow areas" or "about half yellow."

Results The banana in the closed bag changes from green to yellow first, the banana in the open bag changes color second, and the uncovered banana changes color last.

Why? Assuming the bananas are equal in size and ripeness, they give off the same amount of ethylene gas. This gas causes the bananas to ripen. The skin of a banana changes from green to yellow then to brown as the fruit ripens. As the fruit ripens, it produces even more ethylene gas. The greater the concentration of ethylene gas around the fruit, the faster it ripens. Covered or uncovered, the ethylene gas produced by the banana causes the fruit to ripen. If uncovered, the gas diffuses (spreads out in all directions) into the air, so the concentration of ethylene gas is low. In the open bag, some of the ethylene gas is collected and some of it is diffused, so there is a moderate concentration of gas. In the closed bag, the gas is trapped, so the banana in this bag is exposed to the greatest concentration of ethylene gas and ripens the fastest.

Solutions to Exercises

1. *Think!*

   - Ethylene gas causes fruit to ripen.

   - Fruit produces more ethylene gas as it ripens.

   - Placing fruit together speeds up the ripening process because there is more ethylene gas present.

   The fruit in figure A will ripen faster.

2. *Think!*

   - Weeds are plants that grow where they are not wanted.

   - A farmer wants only corn to grow in his corn field.

   Figure B represents the sunflower as a weed.

25
Stringy
Textile Engineering

What You Need to Know

Textile engineering is the branch of engineering concerned with the design, development, and production of textile products. **Textiles** are materials used in making fabrics as well as the fabrics that are made. A **fabric** is a material made by **weaving** (interlacing), **knitting** (interlocking loops of thread) or **felting** (matting together) threads. A **thread** is a cord made by twisting together **fibers** (single strands of material).

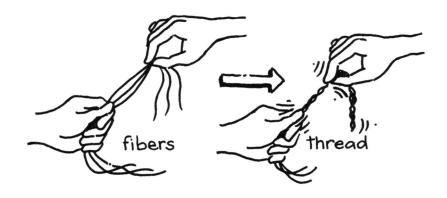

fibers → thread

Fabric is most commonly used to make clothes. Other uses include making materials for lifesaving artificial blood vessels, space travel, parachutes, flags, and sports equipment such as footballs and trampolines. Natural fibers come from plants and animals. For example, cotton fiber is from a cotton plant, wool fibers come from sheep, and silk fiber is made by silkworms. **Synthetic** (man-made) fibers include nylon, rayon, and polyester. Many synthetic fibers are made from petroleum.

In designing fabrics, textile engineers consider the different qualities of different types of threads and fibers. Some are weak and break easily, whereas others are strong and difficult to break. Characteristics of fabrics that determine which fibers are used for specific purposes include softness, durability, elasticity, absorbency, and insulation. **Softness** is a measure of how easily a fabric can be squeezed together. Durability is a measure of the length of time a fabric remains useful. **Elasticity** is a measure of how much a material can be stretched and still return to its original shape. **Absorbency** is a measure of how much fluid a fabric can take in and hold. Insulation is a measure of how well a fabric restricts the flow of energy such as heat. Insulating materials are good for making winter clothes because heat is poorly transferred through it. This means they tend to hold body heat next to the body, keeping you warm.

Chemicals are sometimes added to fabrics to give them specific characteristics such as being water resistant or fire resistant. **Water resistant** means the ability to keep water away. Water-resistant materials do not easily absorb water. Rain gear, tents, luggage, and umbrellas are made of water-resistant fabrics. While most water-resistant materials have some kind of coating, some fabrics are water resistant because the fibers are very small, which allows the weaving to be so tight that water is easily wiped off before it can sink into the fabric. Fabrics that are **fire resistant** are treated with chemicals so that they don't burn as easily.

Textile engineers have a never-ending job of testing and designing new materials for everyday use as well as for special jobs—for example, space suits for astronauts. The materials for space suits must protect astronauts against the dangers of space. Each suit has many layers of material. The outer layers protect astronauts from the heat of the Sun. The underlying layers keep the suit airtight. There is no oxygen in space, so the suit has to hold breathable air in it. A leak in the suit could be deadly. Of course, the inside layers of the suit must keep astronauts comfortable.

Exercises

1. Choose the word that best describes the fabric of a towel.

   a. water-resistant

   b. absorbent

   c. insulating

2. Choose the word that best describes the fabric in an umbrella.

   a. water resistant

   b. absorbent

   c. insulating

Activity: STRONGER

Purpose To compare the strength of a single fiber with threads made of different numbers of fibers.

Materials 12-inch (30-cm) piece of embroidery thread with 6 or more strands
transparent tape
2 pencils

Procedure

1. Separate one strand from the embroidery thread.

2. Tape one end of the strand to one of the pencils, then wrap the strand around the pencil two or three times.

3. Repeat step 2 using the free end of the strand and the second pencil.

4. Hold one pencil in each hand and pull the pencils apart so that the strand is taut. Now try to break the strand by pulling on the pencils. Notice how easy or difficult it is to break the strand.

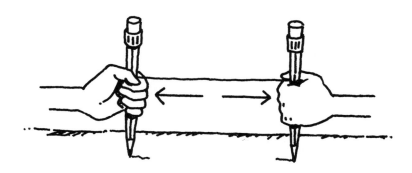

5. Separate two strands from the embroidery thread.

6. Twist the strands together, then repeat steps 2 through 4.

7. Repeat step 6 using three strands.

Results The single strand is easily broken. Two strands are difficult to break, and three generally cannot be broken.

Why? A single strand of fiber is called a **ply**. Thread with two strands twisted together is called 2-ply. Three strands twisted together is called 3-ply. Using two or more strands to make thread makes it stronger and more durable. As the number of strands increases, the strength of the thread increases. Thus, 3-ply thread is stronger than 2-ply.

Solutions to Exercises

1. *Think!*

   - Towels are used to dry wet things.

   - Absorbent means to take in water.

   b. Towels are made of absorbent material.

2. *Think!*

   - Umbrellas are used to keep water off of things.

   - Water resistance is the ability to keep water away.

   - Water-resistant materials do not easily absorb water.

   a. An umbrella is made of water-resistant material.

Glossary

absorb Taken in.

absorbency A measure of how much fluid a fabric can take in and hold.

accelerate To increase the speed of an object; to speed up.

acoustical engineering The branch of engineering dealing with acoustics.

acoustics How sound behaves in and is affected by a structure.

advection The movement of water in any form through the atmosphere.

aerodynamics The study of the forces on objects due to their motion through a fluid as well as the motion of the fluid on them.

aeronautical engineering The branch of engineering concerned with the design, manufacturing, and operation of aircraft.

aerospace engineering The branch of engineering concerned with the design, manufacture, and operation of launch vehicles, satellites, spacecraft, and ground support facilities for the exploration of outer space.

agricultural engineering The branch of engineering concerned with the production of agricultural products in the quantity and quality needed by today's consumers.

agriculture   The raising of plants and animals for food, feed, fiber, fuel, and other useful products.

air   The name of the mixture of gases in Earth's atmosphere.

aircraft   A vehicle that can move through the air.

airfoil   A surface designed to produce lift and drag forces from air flowing around it.

air pressure   The force of air on surfaces due to the motion of air molecules.

allelochemicals   Chemicals that inhibit the growth of plants.

alloy   A mixture of two or more metals or a mixture of one or more metals and a nonmetal, particularly carbon.

altitude   The height above sea level.

anemometer   An instrument used to measure the speed of wind.

atmosphere   The layer of air surrounding Earth.

atom   The basic building block of all substances.

atomic mass   The sum of the protons and neutrons in an atom's nucleus.

atomic number   The number of protons in an atom's nucleus.

attract   To pull together.

balanced forces   Two equal forces acting in opposite directions on an object.

barometer   An instrument used to measure air pressure.

battery   A device that changes chemical energy into electric energy.

Bernoulli's principle   The statement that the pressure of a fluid on a surface over which it flows decreases as its speed increases.

binoculars   An optical instrument used to assist the eye in seeing distant objects.

biodegradable   Capable of being decomposed by micro-organisms.

biological engineering   The branch of engineering concerned with designing methods and products that will create a more healthful living environment for people, animals, and plants.

biology   The study of living things.

bond   An attractive force between atoms.

brittle   Easily broken.

bronze   An alloy made of two metals: tin and copper.

buoyancy   The ability to float.

burning   An oxidation reaction; also called combustion.

casting   The forming of metals into specific shapes by pouring molten metal into molds.

centrifugal force   An apparent center-fleeing force due to the inertia of an object moving in a curved path.

centripetal force   The force on an object moving in a curved path that is directed toward the center of the curve.

chain reaction   A nuclear reaction in which the material that starts the reaction is also one of the products. The reaction continues until there is no more material that can or does react.

chasing   The process of pushing a pattern into a malleable metal's surface.

chemical   A substance made of one or more elements.

chemical energy   The energy released when a chemical bond is broken.

chemical engineering The branch of engineering concerned with the chemical properties of substances and how they can be used to make products and packaging for products.

chemical metallurgist An engineer who is concerned with the chemical properties of metals and the chemical processes that relate to metals.

chemical properties The characteristics of a chemical that determines how it chemically reacts.

chemical reaction Occurs when one chemical or a mixture of two or more chemicals change to form one or more new chemicals.

clay The smallest soil particles; soil particles that are less than 0.002 mm in diameter.

closed circuit A circuit with no breaks in its path, so electricity will flow through it.

cloud A visible mass of water drops that float in the atmosphere.

collagen A fibrous protein that connects, strengthens, and supports various parts of the body including the skin and bones.

combustion An oxidation reaction; also called burning.

compact To press together.

compress To push together.

concave lens A lens with a surface that curves inward like the bowl of a spoon; diverges light passing through it.

condense The process of changing from a gas to a liquid.

conduct To transfer.

conductivity The ability of a substance to allow either electricity or heat to easily pass through it.

control rod   A rod in a nuclear reactor made of material such as cadmium, boron, and carbon that can absorb neutrons. Control rods can be raised or lowered to control the number of neutrons available to react. The number of neutrons affects the number of reactions that occur. Thus, control rods control the energy produced in the reactor.

converge   In reference to light, it means light rays bend toward and meet at a single point located on the normal.

convex lens   A lens with a surface that curves outward like the surface of a ball; converges light passing through it; a magnifying lens.

corrugated   To have grooves and ridges.

crops   The yield from plants in a single growing season.

crude oil   A natural nonrenewable energy resource.

cumulative   To add up.

current electricity   Electricity due to the motion of free electrons.

dead forces   The weight of permanent objects in or on a structure.

decelerate   To decrease the speed of an object; to slow down.

decomposition   A chemical reaction in which chemicals break apart, forming smaller chemicals.

deform   To change the shape of a material.

dense   Describes many particles of a substance in a small space.

density   A physical property comparing the mass of a certain volume of a substance.

diffuse   To scatter in many directions.

diverge   In reference to light, it means light rays bend away from the principal axis.

drag   A friction force in the direction opposite of thrust.

drawing   The process of shaping a metal into a wire by pulling it through a hole.

ductility   The ability of a substance to be drawn into a wire.

durability   A measure of how long a product keeps its original qualities and usefulness.

earthquake   A shaking of the ground caused by a sudden movement of rock beneath Earth's surface.

earthquake engineering   The branch of engineering concerned with the effects of earthquakes, including reducing harmful effects of earthquakes on structures such as roads, bridges, and buildings.

echo   A reflected sound wave.

elastic deformation   The deformation of a material while being stressed.

elasticity   The ability of a material to return to its original size and shape after being deformed.

elastic limit   The maximum force that will cause elastic deformation. Past this limit, the material is permanently deformed.

electrical engineering   The branch of engineering concerned with designing things and systems that makes electricity useful.

electric charge   The property of particles that causes a force between them; positive and negative.

electric circuit   A pathway for electricity.

electric conduction   The transfer of electricity due to the movement of free electrons in a material.

electric conductor   A material that easily conducts electricity; has many free electrons; a metal.

electricity   A form of energy produced by the presence of or the movement of electric charges.

electromagnetic spectrum   All the types of radiant energy listed in order of their energy level.

electromagnetic waves   Radiant energy waves.

electron   The negatively charged particle outside the nucleus of an atom.

elements   Substances made of one kind of atom.

energy   The ability to do work. *See also* **kinetic energy** and **potential energy**.

engineering   A profession that applies knowledge of science, mathematics, and experience to produce something or a process that is useful.

environment   The surroundings of an organism; that is, living and nonliving things that affect the life, development, and survival of an organism.

environmental engineering   The branch of engineering concerned with designing things and processes to improve the environment.

enzyme   A protein that controls chemical reactions in living organisms by causing reactions and changing how fast those reactions occur.

epicenter   The point on Earth's surface directly above the hypocenter.

erosion   The breakdown and removal of a material's particles by natural processes, such as water and wind.

etch   To form a pattern on a metal's surface by cutting away part of the surface.

evaporation   The process of a liquid changing into a gas.

expand   The separation of material particles, resulting in an increase in size.

eyeglasses   An optical instrument that allows a person to clearly see objects at distances that appear blurry without them.

fabric   A material made by weaving, knitting, or felting threads.

fatigue   Commonly means weakness because of repeated motion.

fatigue life   The number of deforming cycles of motion that a material can endure before breaking.

fatigue resistance   The resistance of a material to breaking due to material fatigue.

felting   Making a fabric by matting threads together.

fibers   Single strands of material.

fire protection engineering   The branch of engineering concerned with designing systems and equipment that prevent or combat fire, such as sprinkler systems in buildings as well as firefighting equipment used by firefighters.

fire resistant   Harder to burn.

flex   To bend back and forth.

flight   The action of an object moving through the air.

flow rate   A measure of the volume of liquid flowing through an opening in a given period of time.

fluid   A gas or a liquid.

fluorescence   The process in which special chemicals capture ultraviolet radiation and change it into visible light, which is emitted.

fluorescent brightening agent   A chemical that cause fluorescence; also called an optical brightening agent.

focal point   Where light rays meet.

force   A push or a pull on an object.

forging   The hammering or pressing of a metal in order to shape it.

free electrons   Electrons that are not tightly bound to a single atom and are relatively free to move from one atom to another in a material.

friction   The force that resists the motion of objects in contact with each other.

fuel   A material that can burn.

garbage   Solid indoor waste, as from businesses, schools, and homes.

gelatin   A protein obtained from animal tissues.

geotechnical engineering   The branch of engineering concerned with properties of the ground in regions where man-made structures such as buildings, roadways, tunnels, and bridges will be built.

gluten   A protein found in grains.

gravity   (1) The force pulling any object downward, which is toward the center of Earth; a force perpendicular to Earth's surface. (2) In reference to a structure, it is the sum of the dead and live forces acting on the structure.

groundwater   Underground water; the source of water for some wells and springs.

hydraulic engineering   The branch of engineering concerned with the flow and transporting of fluids, primarily water.

hydrology engineering The branch of engineering concerned with water in Earth's atmosphere as well as water on and beneath Earth's surface.

hypocenter The spot below Earth's surface where vibrations from an earthquake begin.

ignite To catch on fire.

image A representation of a physical object formed by lenses or mirrors.

immiscible A quality describing the inability of two liquids to mix and blend together—for example, oil and water.

incinerate To burn something until it turns to ash.

inertia The tendency of an object at rest to remain at rest and an object in motion to remain in motion.

infiltration The process by which water moves from the surface into the ground.

infrared radiation (IR) A type of radiant energy that is invisible and is sensed by your skin as heat; also called heat waves.

insulation A measure of how well a fabric restricts the flow of energy through it; any material that inhibits the transfer of energy through it.

intensity In reference to the Mercalli scale, it is a measure of the amount of destruction of structures and the deaths and injuries of people caused by an earthquake.

interception The process by which precipitation collects on the surface of objects such as plants and buildings and eventually evaporates without reaching the ground.

kindling temperature The minimum temperature at which a substance will burn.

kinetic energy   The energy of moving objects.

knitting   Making a fabric by interlocking loops of thread.

landfill   An area where waste is buried.

lateral force   A force directed at the side of a structure.

lateral vibration   Movement from side to side.

leachate   Liquid that percolates through a material.

lens   A shaped piece of transparent material that changes the direction of light passing through it.

lift   The upward force on aircraft.

lightning   A visible static discharge between clouds and other objects such as Earth, buildings, or people.

live forces   The weight of temporary objects, including people, in or on a structure.

magnitude   In reference to earthquakes, the amount of energy released by an earthquake.

malleablility   The ability of a substance to be deformed, especially by hammering or the ability of a substance to be rolled into a thin sheet.

mass   A physical property; the amount of substance making up an object.

material fatigue   The weakening of a material often to the point of breaking because of repeated motion.

melt   The process of a solid changing to a liquid as a result of an increase in temperature.

Mercalli scale   A measurement of an earthquake's intensity. *See also* intensity.

metallurgical engineering   The branch of engineering concerned with metals.

metallurgy   The science of metals, including understanding their chemical and physical properties, how to remove them from rocks and minerals, and their uses.

metals   Elements that are usually shiny solids that can be formed into sheets or wires and are good conductors of heat and electricity.

meteorological engineering   The branch of engineering concerned with designing and testing meteorological equipment used for sensing, detecting, measuring, recording, and displaying weather conditions.

meteorology   The study of weather.

microscope   An optical instrument that assists in seeing things too small for the unaided eye to see clearly.

mirror   A device with a surface that reflects light.

miscibility   A physical property describing the ability of a substance to mix with and thoroughly blend with another substance.

mixture   Two or more substances that are combined but keep their own identity; *see* **solutions**.

molten   Liquid form.

neutrons   Nucleons without a charge.

Newton's first law of motion   A statement explaining inertia.

Newton's second law of motion   A statement explaining how the force needed to accelerate an object depends on the mass of the object.

Newton's third law of motion   A statement explaining that every force on an objects results in an equal force in the opposite direction. These pairs of forces are called action-reaction pairs and act on different objects.

nonrenewable energy resource A source of energy that is not replaceable and can be used up, such as crude oil.

nuclear energy The energy released during a nuclear reaction.

nuclear engineering The branch of engineering concerned with nuclear energy.

nuclear fission A type of nuclear reaction in which a large nucleus is bombarded by a fast-moving neutron, causing the nucleus to split into roughly two equal parts with the release of large amounts of energy and usually two or more fast-moving neutrons.

nuclear reaction Occurs when there is any change in an atom's nucleus.

nuclear reactor A device in which controlled nuclear fission reactions occur and the released energy is used to heat water. The heat energy from the water is transferred to other devices that use it to produce electricity.

nucleon Any particle in an atom's nucleus.

nucleus The center part of an atom where some of its atomic particles including protons group together.

nutrient Any substance that living organisms need to grow, produce energy, and stay healthy.

opaque The physical property of a material describing the radiant energy it blocks; commonly used to describe materials that block visible light; cannot be seen through.

open circuit A circuit with a break in its path, so electricity will not flow through it.

open landfill An open hole where waste is dumped.

optical Anything dealing with sight or light.

optical brightening agent *See* **fluorescent brightening agent**.

optical engineering The branch of engineering concerned with designing, constructing, and testing optical instruments.

optical instrument A device that directs the path of light in order to better assist sight.

oxidation reaction A chemical reaction between a substance and oxygen that produces heat.

oxygen A gas in air that does not burn itself but is needed for other substances to burn.

papain An enzyme extracted from papaya, a tropical fruit; a common enzyme in meat tenderizer; digests gelatin.

percolate To move through the spaces in a material.

petroleum A common name for crude oil and any of its products.

petroleum engineering The branch of engineering concerned with discovering underground regions containing crude oil as well as natural gas.

physical metallurgist An engineer who studies the physical properties of metals and their alloys to determine the best methods of processing them into useful products.

ply A single strand of fiber.

pollution Anything that destroys the purity of a substance, making it not useful.

pores Spaces between the particles of a material.

porosity A measure of how porous a material is.

porous The quality of a material having spaces between its particles.

potential energy Stored energy; the energy of objects

raised above a surface due to the force of gravity pulling on them.

precipitation   Liquid and solid forms of water that fall from the atmosphere.

principal axis   In reference to a lens or curved mirror, it is an imaginary line passing through the center.

process metallurgist   An engineer who develops and improves metalworking processes such as casting, forging, rolling, and drawing.

product   The substance produced in a chemical reaction.

product development engineering   The branch of engineering concerned with designing, developing, and testing new products.

product durability engineering   The branch of engineering concerned with designs and processes responsible for product durability.

proteins   One type of nutrient.

proton   The positive particle inside the nucleus of an atom; nucleon with a positive charge.

radiant energy   *See* **radiation**.

radiation   Energy that travels in waves, such as visible light and ultraviolet radiation.

reactant   The starting substance in a chemical reaction.

recycle   To make new products from old ones.

refining   In reference to a metal, it is the removal of any impurities combined with a metal.

reflect   To bounce off of a surface.

repel   To push apart.

residue   The solid part left behind when a mixture is filtered.

Richter scale   A number system used to measure the magnitude of an earthquake.

rocket   An aircraft that is powered by gases forced out of one end.

roller-coaster engineering   The branch of engineering concerned with designing, constructing, and testing roller-coaster cars and the path they follow.

rolling   The process of shaping a metal into a smooth, flat sheet by moving it between rollers.

runoff   The liquid water from precipitation that is unable to soak into the ground and that moves over its surface.

sand   The largest soil particles; soil particles with a diameter of 0.05 mm for fine sand to 2.0 mm for very coarse sand.

sanitary landfill   A landfill with a liner and waste that is daily covered with a layer of dirt.

science   A method of discovering the composition and behavior of the physical world; a study of the natural world.

silt   Medium-size soil particles; soil particles between 0.002 and 0.05 mm in size.

softness   A measure of how easily a fabric can be squeezed together.

soil texture   The physical property of soil describing the size of its particles. *See also* **clay**; **sand**; **silt**.

solar energy   Radiant energy from the Sun.

solar engineering   The branch of engineering concerned with designing structures and processes to capture and use solar energy.

solid waste   Garbage and yard waste.

solute   The part of a solution that dissolves.

solution   A mixture of a solute and a solvent.

solvent   The part of a solution that a solute dissolves in.

sound   Wave energy produced and transferred by vibrating material such as air; also called sound waves; a sensation interpreted by the brain.

sound waves   *See* **sound**.

static discharge   The loss of static electricity that occurs when electrons are transferred to another material.

static electricity   A type of electricity due to the buildup of stationary electric charges.

stress   The force on an area of an object that tends to deform it.

stress engineering   The branch of engineering concerned with designing materials with high elastic limits as well as high tensile strengths. Stress engineers also design methods for testing these stress limits.

structural engineering   The branch of engineering concerned with designing and constructing structures such as buildings, bridges, and dams.

synthetic   Man-made.

telescope   An optical instrument used to assist the eye in seeing distant objects.

temperature   How hot or cold a material is.

tensile strength   The maximum amount of stretching force that a material can withstand without breaking.

textile engineering   The branch of engineering concerned with the design, development, and production of textile products.

textiles   The materials used in making fabrics as well as the fabrics that are made.

thermometer   An instrument used for measuring temperature.

thread   A cord made by twisting together fibers.

thrust   The force on an aircraft that moves it forward.

translucent   The physical property of a material describing the scattering of radiant energy that passes through it; generally used to describe materials that scatter visible light passing through them. Objects viewed through translucent materials look blurry.

transparent   The physical property of a material that allows visible light to easily pass through.

transpiration   The process by which water is lost through the surface of plants.

twist   To wind.

ultrasound   Sound vibrations above the normal range of human hearing.

ultraviolet radiation (UV)   Invisible radiant energy that can cause your skin to tan, but in excess it can damage your skin.

unbalanced force   The force resulting from the sum of unequal forces acting on an object.

vapor   The gas form of a substance that is usually in liquid form.

vaporize   The process of a substance changing into a gas.

variable   Things that can change.

vertical force   A force directed up or down on a structure.

vertical vibration   Up-and-down movement.

vibration   A back-and-forth or to-and-fro motion.

viscosity   A measure of the ability of a fluid to flow; the higher the viscosity, the slower the fluid flows.

visible light   The only type of radiant energy that the human eye can see. *See also* **visible spectrum**.

visible spectrum   The different types of visible light listed in order of their energy. The colors of light making up the visible spectrum listed from least to greatest energy are red, orange, yellow, green, blue, indigo, and violet.

volume   The amount of space occupied by a substance.

waste   Things that are not wanted.

waste disposal   The process of getting rid of unwanted things.

water cycle   The processes involved in the movement of water between Earth and its atmosphere.

water resistant   The ability to keep water away.

weather   The changes in conditions in Earth's lower atmosphere.

weaving   Making a fabric by interlacing threads.

weed   Any plant that grows where it is not wanted.

weight   A physical property; a measure of the amount of gravity pulling on an object.

wind   Horizontal movement of air in relation to Earth's surface.

work   The results of an unbalanced force causing an object to move; applying a force over a distance; equal to the energy of a moving object; equal to the product of a force times the distance the force is applied.

yard waste   Outdoor solid waste such as grass and sticks.

Index

absorb, 35, 44, 177
absorbency, 172, 177
accelerate, 12, 177
acoustical engineering, 43–49,
    177
  activity, 47–48
  definition of, 43, 177
acoustics, 43, 177
advection, 160, 177
aerodynamics, 19, 177
aeronautical engineering,
    19–25, 177
  activity, 22–25
  definition of, 19, 177
aerospace engineering, 11–17,
    177
  activity, 15–17
  definition of, 11, 177
agricultural engineering,
    165–169, 177
  activity, 174–175
  definition of, 165, 177
agriculture, 165, 177
air, 19, 178
aircraft, 19, 178
airfoil, 20, 178
air pressure, 151, 178
allelochemicals, 165, 178
alloy
  bronze, 107, 179
  definition of, 107, 178

altitude, 151, 178
anemometer
  activity, 154–156
  definition of, 152, 178
Archytas, 11
atmosphere, 19, 178
atom
  definition of, 51, 178
  electron, 51, 183
  neutron, 73, 188
  nucleons, 73, 189
  nucleus, 51, 73, 189
  proton, 51, 191
atomic mass, 73, 178
atomic number, 73, 178
attract, 51, 178

balanced forces, 12, 178
barometer, 151, 178
battery, 52, 178
Bernoulli's principle, 29,
    178
binoculars, 59, 179
biodegradable, 126, 179
biological engineering,
    101–105, 179
  activity, 104–105
  definition of, 101,
    179
biology, 101, 179
bond, 81, 179